Leader's G

God • Good News • Bible • Jesus Christ • Church • Living this Life • Eternal Life

7 Things Christians Believe

Creeds and Deeds, Part I

Jeff Rasche

FAITH in Motion

 Abingdon Press

This book is printed on acid-free, recycled paper.

03 04 05 06 07 08 09 10 11 12—10 9 8 7 6 5 4 3 2 1

MANUFACTURED IN THE UNITED STATES OF AMERICA

Development Team
Jola Bortner
Rusty Cartee
Harriette Cross
Tim Gossett
Sharon Meads
Beth Miller
David Stewart

Editorial Team
Crystal A. Zinkiewicz, Senior Editor
Tim Gossett, Development Editor
Josh Tinley, Associate Editor

Design Team
Keely J. Moore, Design Manager
Kelly Chinn, Designer

Administrative Staff
Neil M. Alexander, Publisher
Harriet Jane Olson, Vice President/Editor of Church School Resources
Bob Shell, Director of Youth Resources

CONTENTS

Session 1: We Believe the Good News 7

Session 2: We Believe the Bible 13

Session 3: We Believe in God 19

Session 4: We Believe in Jesus Christ 25

Session 5: We Believe in the Church 31

Session 6: We Believe in Living This Life . . .37

Session 7: We Believe in Eternal Life 43

Reproducible Pages 49

I Think, I Wonder, I Believe Retreat 58

Worship in an Eggshell .61

Out and About: Visit a Christian Bookstore 63

How to Use Faith in Motion

Leader's Guide

Information and Formation

Topic and Key Verse
This Life-to-Bible curriculum starts with important topics for junior highs and goes to God's Word.

Take-Home Learning
The goal for the session is clear.

Younger Youth and This Topic
Find out more about your youth and how they are likely to connect with this concern.

Theology and This Topic
How does Christian faith and tradition help us to understand and deal with the concern?

You and the Scripture
Our being formed as a Christian through Bible reflection and prayer is essential for our teaching.

Transformation

The ultimate goal: Youth will become more fully devoted disciples of Jesus Christ.

We Believe the Good News

Topic: Believe the Good News!

Scripture: Isaiah 61 (especially verses 1-3), Luke 2:8-15; John 3:17

Key Verse: "Do not be afraid; for see—I am bringing you good news of great joy for all the people: to you is born this day in the city of David a Savior, who is the Messiah, the Lord" (Luke 2:10-11).

Take-Home Learning: The Christian faith is good news even in the midst of the worst possible bad news.

Younger Youth and the Topic

Dare we say it? Many youth do not think of the church as good news. Some would rather be sleeping in than stumbling out of bed early on Sunday morning. "Do I have to go to church today?" they ask. Then their mean parents inevitably deliver the bad news: "Yes, you do!"

Even those youth who spring out of bed, shout, "All right! It's Sunday!" and rush to Sunday school are sometimes driven by "good news" that is not of a religious nature. They might recall the last-second shot that gave their basketball team the win last night, the fact that there is no school on Monday, or their excitement about the girl or boy they've had their eye on who just asked them to prom. (Or the girl or boy in Sunday school who they've had their eye on and can't wait to see again.)

The "bad news" of the church does not stop with the early mornings. To some youth, the church and their parents are coconspirators, working to limit their behavior. Adolescents hear plenty of lectures from their parents condemning drinking, smoking, drugs, R-rated movies, staying out past curfew, hanging out with the "wrong crowd," engaging in heavy necking or petting—in other words, just about everything! Many youth feel that the church is just there to tell them what not to do.

Obviously, we need to help youth see beyond the limits their faith imposes so they might discover how their faith can enrich their lives. Some youth feel guilty about past mistakes and present temptations and fear God's anger and judgment. These youth often have the same attitude toward their parents. Therefore, the news that Jesus came not to codemn us but to save us should be presented to youth as good news. In fact, the word *gospel* literally means "good news." The gospel is good news that youth and adults alike need to hear!

Remember that many youth feel lonely, isolated, left out, neglected, depressed, or angry. There are plenty of sad and negative emotions associated with growing up. Youth need to be reminded that Jesus came into the world to be our friend, and that we can trust God to be with us regardless of our circumstances.

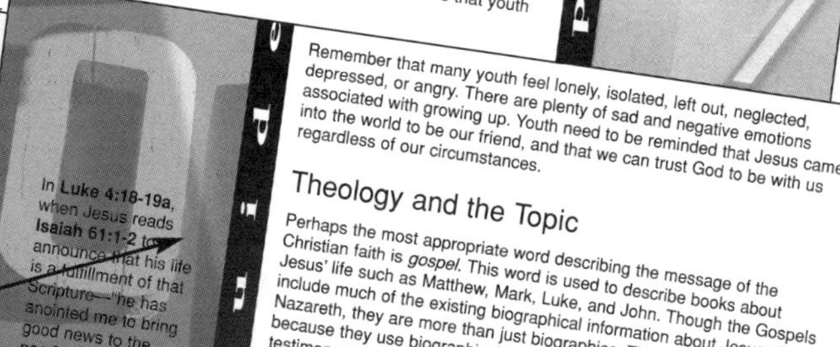

Theology and the Topic

Perhaps the most appropriate word describing the message of the Christian faith is *gospel*. This word is used to describe books about Jesus' life such as Matthew, Mark, Luke, and John. Though the Gospels include much of the existing biographical information about Jesus of Nazareth, they are more than just biographies. They are called "Gospels" because they use biographical narratives and information to present a testimony of faith and a theological message for the reader. As John wrote near the end of his Gospel, "These [signs] are written so that you may come to believe that Jesus is the Messiah, the Son of God, and that through believing you may have life in his name" (John 20:31).

Perhaps the third verse of "Hark! The Herald Angels Sing" does the best job of putting the gospel into a few simple words: "Light and life to all he brings, risen with healing in his wings. Mild he lays his glory by, born that we no more may die, born to raise us from the earth, born to give us second birth." Many Christmas carols beautifully express this good news of our Christian faith.

As Jesus himself said in John's Gospel (3:17), he did not come into the world to be our judge, but our savior. The name *Jesus* means "God is with us"; this is the good news. Because God is with us we do not need to be afraid of condemnation or punishment. We have a powerful, perfect, and loving friend; we have been rescued from sin and death and have been given the joy of new life in Christ.

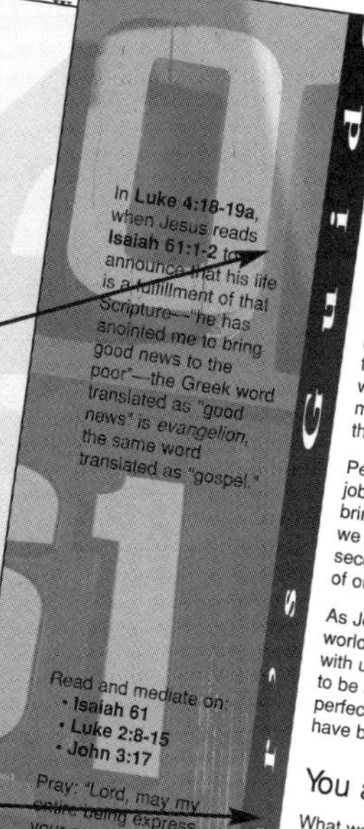

In **Luke 4:18-19a**, when Jesus reads **Isaiah 61:1-2** to announce that his life is a fulfillment of that Scripture—"he has anointed me to bring good news to the poor"—the Greek word translated as "good news" is *evangelion*, the same word translated as "gospel."

Read and mediate on:
- **Isaiah 61**
- **Luke 2:8-15**
- **John 3:17**

Pray: "Lord, may my entire being express your good news. I know that you came to provide for the poor, heal the sick, comfort the grieving, befriend the lonely, and forgive the sinner. For each of these bad situations, you came to bring and to be good news. Thank you for the good news that you have given me too. And help me as I share your good news with these youth. Amen."

You and the Scripture

What was the best news you received this week? What has been the best news you have ever received? How do you celebrate good news? How have you found meaning in the good news of Jesus Christ?

Some people seem to be "good news" people. Maybe they are simply lucky; perhaps they don't recognize the bad things that happen to them. At any rate, these people usually seem upbeat, optimistic, and full of good news. Other people are just the opposite. Maybe they have had one too many bad breaks; perhaps they don't recognize the good in their lives. Either way, these people seem to have run out of good news.

Take a moment to reflect on the good news you have received—not just good fortune, but the good God has done for you through Christ. Regardless of how many bad breaks you have had—and some people have had more than their share of misfortune—God is still on your side.

Remember as you share in this lesson with your youth that God is with you as you teach. Through you God will be present for your students in a special way, too.

Overview Chart
Look here for the big picture of the session. Also note the key activities, just in case time is tight.

Jump Right In!
The opening activity engages youth as they arrive.

Experience It!
Learning activities give youth a common base for making new connections.

Explore Connections
What do the Scriptures have to say? What does this mean for my life?
What is a Christian to do?

Take the Challenge
The learnings are not just for Sunday!

Encounter the Holy
Ritual and mystery, prayer and commitment change hearts.

Student Journal and Reproducible Handouts

Life Focus
Topics deal with issues and concerns important to junior high youth.

Spirit Forming
The journal provides practical help and scriptural encouragement.

Group Friendly
Printed Scripture references, discussion questions, and handouts facilitate participation by individuals and small groups.

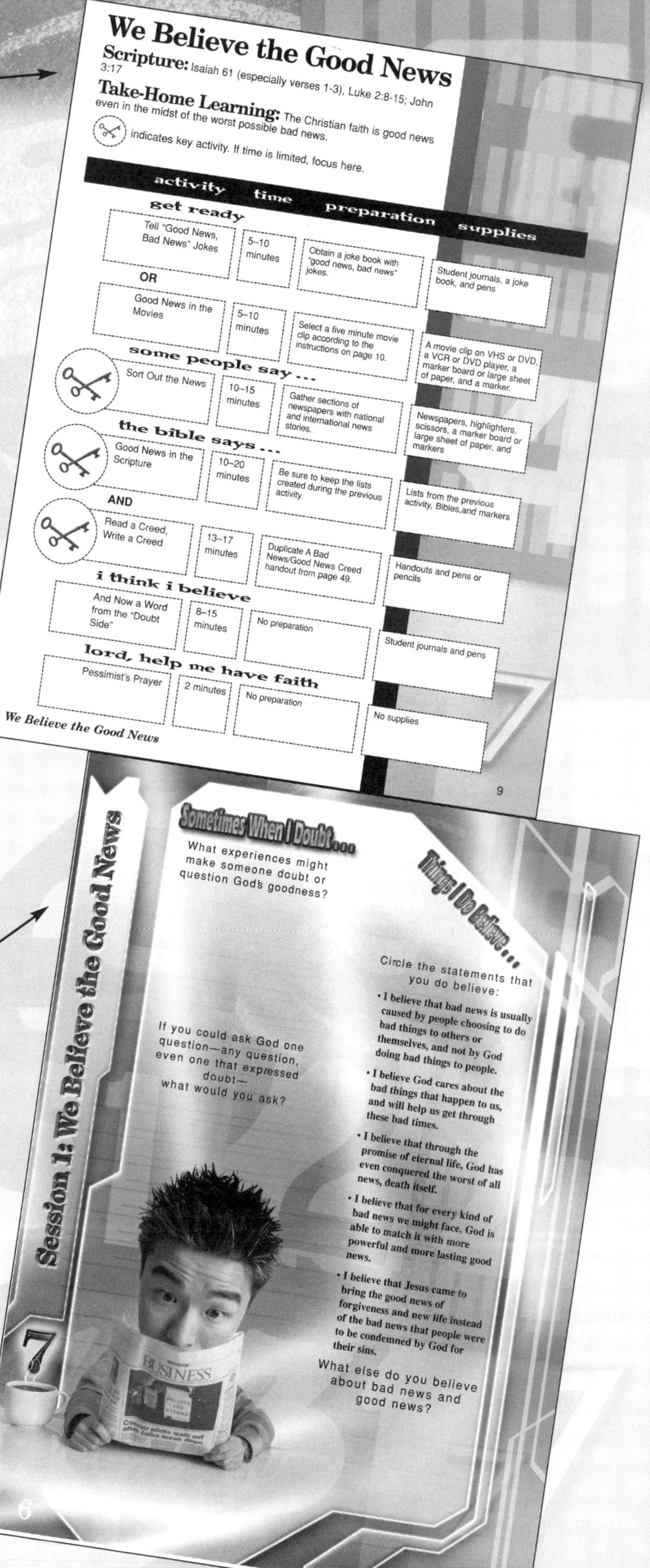

We Believe the Good News

Scripture: Isaiah 61 (especially verses 1-3), Luke 2:8-15; John 3:17

Take-Home Learning: The Christian faith is good news even in the midst of the worst possible bad news.

(key symbol) indicates key activity. If time is limited, focus here.

activity	time	preparation	supplies
get ready			
Tell "Good News, Bad News" Jokes	5–10 minutes	Obtain a joke book with "good news, bad news" jokes.	Student journals, a joke book, and pens
OR			
Good News in the Movies	5–10 minutes	Select a five minute movie clip according to the instructions on page 10.	A movie clip on VHS or DVD, a VCR or DVD player, a marker board or large sheet of paper, and a marker.
some people say . . .			
(key) Sort Out the News	10–15 minutes	Gather sections of newspapers with national and international news stories.	Newspapers, highlighters, scissors, a marker board or large sheet of paper, and markers
the bible says . . .			
(key) Good News in the Scripture	10–20 minutes	Be sure to keep the lists created during the previous activity.	Lists from the previous activity, Bibles, and markers
AND			
(key) Read a Creed, Write a Creed	13–17 minutes	Duplicate A Bad News/Good News Creed handout from page 49.	Handouts and pens or pencils
i think i believe			
And Now a Word from the "Doubt Side"	8–15 minutes	No preparation	Student journals and pens
lord, help me have faith			
Pessimist's Prayer	2 minutes	No preparation	No supplies

We Believe the Good News 9

Session 1: We Believe the Good News

Sometimes When I Doubt . . .
What experiences might make someone doubt or question God's goodness?

If you could ask God one question—any question, even one that expressed doubt—what would you ask?

Things I Do Believe . . .
Circle the statements that you do believe:

- I believe that bad news is usually caused by people choosing to do bad things to others or themselves, and not by God doing bad things to people.
- I believe God cares about the bad things that happen to us, and will help us get through these bad times.
- I believe that through the promise of eternal life, God has even conquered the worst of all news, death itself.
- I believe that for every kind of bad news we might face, God is able to match it with more powerful and more lasting good news.
- I believe that Jesus came to bring the good news of forgiveness and new life instead of the bad news that people were to be condemned by God for their sins.

What else do you believe about bad news and good news?

6 7

Creed: Not Just a Rock Band

In a world where science and technology shape so many aspects of our lives, Christians often have trouble finding value in ancient creeds such as the Apostles' Creed or the Nicene Creed. Many Christian youth may embrace certain elements of these creeds while struggling with others. Some may ask, "If I want to be a true Christian, do I have to believe all of this stuff?" while others metaphorically "cross their fingers" as they stand up and recite these declarations of faith.

Put simply, creeds represent the efforts of the church throughout history to capture the essential elements of the faith. In succinct phrases, creeds have codified what the scholars and religious leaders of a certain time and place held to be religious truth. However, the creeds commonly recited in worship are not directly from the Bible, and there is nothing to prevent us from developing creeds more appropriate to our time and place. In fact, doing so can be a truly fruitful exercise.

By helping youth articulate what they hold true right now, you're helping them form the foundation of a faith that can grow and change as they do.

Throughout this volume, you'll consistently be exploring ancient and modern creeds and statements of faith with your youth. The youth will analyze and criticize these statements, and will have opportunities to develop creeds of their own. You can be a tremendous help to the youth by encouraging them, recognizing that each is at a different point along his or her faith journey, and acknowledging their very important doubts. Where youth are today spiritually is probably not where they will be four, fourteen, or forty years from now. By helping youth articulate what they hold true right now, you're helping them form the foundation of a faith that can grow and change as they do.

Martin Marty, probably the most important sociologist of religion during the past forty years, was once asked how he could say the creeds when he didn't believe some of the statements in them. His response? "I can't say the creeds, but I can sing them." In other words, the creeds tap Martin's emotions and express something deep within him, even though he doesn't consider them intellectual statements of his personal, systematic theology. Likewise, our goal should be not only to help youth to start to carefully and intentionally articulate their faith, but also to help them "sing" along with Christians all around the world that which unites us—a common faith in Jesus Christ.

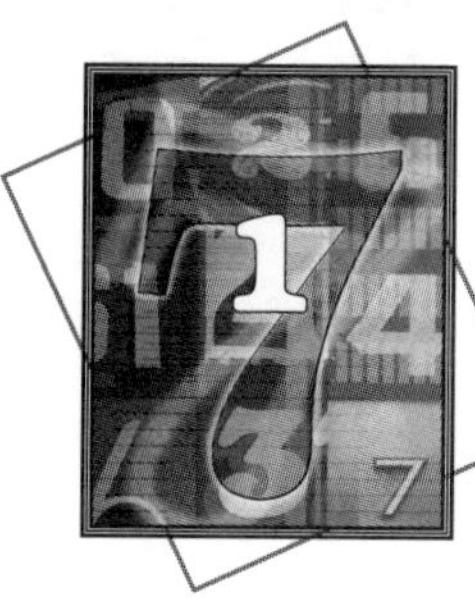

We Believe the Good News

Topic: Believe the Good News!

Scripture: Isaiah 61 (especially verses 1-3), Luke 2:8-15; John 3:17

Key Verse: "Do not be afraid; for see—I am bringing you good news of great joy for all the people: to you is born this day in the city of David a Savior, who is the Messiah, the Lord" (Luke 2:10-11).

Take-Home Learning: The Christian faith is good news even in the midst of the worst possible bad news.

Younger Youth and the Topic

Dare we say it? Many youth do not think of the church as good news. Some would rather be sleeping in than stumbling out of bed early on Sunday morning. "Do I have to go to church today?" they ask. Then their mean parents inevitably deliver the bad news: "Yes, you do!"

Even those youth who spring out of bed, shout, "All right! It's Sunday!" and rush to Sunday school are sometimes driven by "good news" that is not of a religious nature. They might recall the last-second shot that gave their basketball team the win last night, the fact that there is no school on Monday, or their excitement about the girl or boy they've had their eye on who just asked them to prom (or the girl or boy in Sunday school who they've had their eye on and can't wait to see again).

The "bad news" of the church does not stop with the early mornings. To some youth, the church and their parents are coconspirators, working to limit their behavior. Adolescents hear plenty of lectures from their parents condemning drinking, smoking, drugs, R-rated movies, staying out past curfew, hanging out with the "wrong crowd," engaging in heavy necking or petting—in other words, just about everything! Many youth feel that the church is just there to tell them what not to do.

Obviously, we need to help youth see beyond the limits their faith imposes so they might discover how their faith can enrich their lives. Some youth feel guilty about past mistakes and present temptations and fear God's anger and judgment. These youth often have the same attitude toward their parents. Therefore, the news that Jesus came not to codemn us but to save us should be presented to youth as good news. In fact, the word *gospel* literally means "good news." The gospel is good news that youth and adults alike need to hear!

Remember that many youth feel lonely, isolated, left out, neglected, depressed, or angry. There are plenty of sad and negative emotions associated with growing up. Youth need to be reminded that Jesus came into the world to be our friend, and that we can trust God to be with us regardless of our circumstances.

Theology and the Topic

Perhaps the most appropriate word describing the message of the Christian faith is *gospel*. This word is used to describe books about Jesus' life such as Matthew, Mark, Luke, and John. Though the Gospels include much of the existing biographical information about Jesus of Nazareth, they are more than just biographies. They are called "Gospels" because they use biographical narratives and information to present a testimony of faith and a theological message for the reader. As John wrote near the end of his Gospel, "These [signs] are written so that you may come to believe that Jesus is the Messiah, the Son of God, and that through believing you may have life in his name" (John 20:31).

Perhaps the third verse of "Hark! The Herald Angels Sing" does the best job of putting the gospel into a few simple words: "Light and life to all he brings, risen with healing in his wings. Mild he lays his glory by, born that we no more may die, born to raise us from the earth, born to give us second birth." Many Christmas carols beautifully express this good news of our Christian faith.

As Jesus himself said in John's Gospel (3:17), he did not come into the world to be our judge, but our savior. The name *Jesus* means "God is with us"; this is the good news. Because God is with us we do not need to be afraid of condemnation or punishment. We have a powerful, perfect, and loving friend; we have been rescued from sin and death and have been given the joy of new life in Christ.

In **Luke 4:18-19a**, when Jesus reads **Isaiah 61:1-2** to announce that his life is a fulfillment of that Scripture—"he has anointed me to bring good news to the poor"—the Greek word translated as "good news" is *evangelion*, the same word translated as "gospel."

You and the Scripture

What was the best news you received this week? What has been the best news you have ever received? How do you celebrate good news? How have you found meaning in the good news of Jesus Christ?

Some people seem to be "good news" people. Maybe they are simply lucky; perhaps they don't recognize the bad things that happen to them. At any rate, these people usually seem upbeat, optimistic, and full of good news. Other people are just the opposite. Maybe they have had one too many bad breaks; perhaps they don't recognize the good in their lives. Either way, these people seem to have run out of good news.

Take a moment to reflect on the good news you have received—not just good fortune, but the good God has done for you through Christ. Regardless of how many bad breaks you have had—and some people have had more than their share of misfortune—God is still on your side.

Remember as you share in this lesson with your youth that God is with you as you teach. Through you God will be present for your students in a special way, too.

Read and mediate on:

- **Isaiah 61**
- **Luke 2:8-15**
- **John 3:17**

Pray: "Lord, may my entire being express your good news. I know that you came to provide for the poor, heal the sick, comfort the grieving, befriend the lonely, and forgive the sinner. For each of these bad situations, you came to bring and to be good news. Thank you for the good news that you have given me too. and help me as I share your good news with these youth. Amen."

We Believe the Good News

Scripture: Isaiah 61 (especially verses 1-3), Luke 2:8-15; John 3:17

Take-Home Learning: The Christian faith is good news even in the midst of the worst possible bad news.

 indicates key activity. If time is limited, focus here.

activity	time	preparation	supplies
get ready			
Tell "Good News, Bad News" Jokes	5–10 minutes	Obtain a joke book with "good news, bad news" jokes.	Student journals, a joke book, and pens
OR			
Good News in the Movies	5–10 minutes	Select a five minute movie clip according to the instructions on page 10.	A movie clip on VHS or DVD, a VCR or DVD player, a marker board or large sheet of paper, and a marker.
some people say . . .			
Sort Out the News (key activity)	10–15 minutes	Gather sections of newspapers with national and international news stories.	Newspapers, highlighters, scissors, a marker board or large sheet of paper, and markers
the bible says . . .			
Good News in the Scripture (key activity)	10–20 minutes	Be sure to keep the lists created during the previous activity.	Lists from the previous activity, Bibles,and markers
AND			
Read a Creed, Write a Creed (key activity)	13–17 minutes	Duplicate A Bad News/Good News Creed handout from page 49.	Handouts and pens or pencils
i think i believe			
And Now a Word from the "Doubt Side"	8–15 minutes	No preparation	Student journals and pens
lord, help me have faith			
Pessimist's Prayer	2 minutes	No preparation	No supplies

get ready

Provide student journals, a joke book, and pens.

For an example of a "good news, bad news" joke, look at page 4 of the student journal.

Tell "Good News, Bad News" Jokes (5–10 minutes)

Find a joke book with "good news, bad news" jokes, and/or invite the class to complete some of the jokes from "Good News/Bad News Jokes" on pages 4–5 of the student journal. Spend a few minutes telling and/or creating jokes. Then ask:

- How do you look at the good news and bad news in your life? Do you focus too much on one or the other?
- Why do some people think of Christianity as bad news? (*It places limits on what you can do, it can be boring and time consuming, and so on.*)

Say: "Our faith is more about good news than bad news. Today's lesson explores the good news of our faith."

OR

Provide a previewed movie clip on VHS or DVD, a VCR or DVD player, a marker board or large sheet of paper and a marker.

Be sure to read the note on permissions on page 48 and to get permission from each youth's parents before showing any movie clips, especially if the clip includes any potentially objectionable content.

Good News in the Movies (5–10 minutes)

Many movies have a dramatic climax when good news brings hope to characters in an otherwise hopeless situation. For example, in a romantic comedy two lovers are having their differences and appear to be going their separate ways until . . . one of them decides to forgive the other. By the end of the movie, the couple is ready to live happily ever after! In an action movie the good guys (and sometimes entire planets) are about to be destroyed by an evil nemesis until . . . some unlikely hero turns the tables and drives the villain away.

Choose a five-minute movie clip in which hope suddenly saves an otherwise hopeless situation. Show this clip to the students, then ask:

- What bad news made you anxious or kept you in suspense?
- What good news turned the story around?
- How would this story have ended differently if there had not been any good news?

Then ask:

- What are some examples of bad news in the world today?

Write responses to this question on a marker board or large sheet of paper. For each "bad news" situation, ask, "If you could be God for a day, what good news would you provide to bring hope amid each of these bad news situations?"

some people say . . .

Provide newspapers, highlighters, scissors, a marker board or large sheet of paper, and markers.

Sort out the News (10–15 minutes)

Divide the youth into groups of two or three. Give each group a few sections of recent newspapers dealing with national and international news (the main section of a daily paper would work well) and two colors of highlighter markers.

Ask each group to select three or four news stories. Instruct them to read through the stories, highlighting "good news" in one color and "bad news" in the other color. (For example, in a story about an earthquake, the sentences telling about injury and destruction would be highlighted as bad news, sentences telling about the courageous and compassionate efforts of volunteers and rescue workers would be highlighted as good news.) Encourage youth to look for both the bad and the good in each story.

Divide a board or large sheet of paper in two columns, one labeled "bad news," the other labeled "good news." Ask the groups to say something about the stories they selected and the bad and good news in those stories. Record each example of bad news or good news in the appropriate column. Then ask, "In which of these stories did bad news become good news?" Invite the youth to discuss these stories.

Do not remove the columns you create; they will be needed for the next activity.

Good News in the Scripture (10–20 minutes)

the bible says ...

Provide the lists created for the previous activity (on a marker board or large sheet of paper), Bibles, and markers.

Hand out Bibles, and ask a volunteer to read aloud each passage:

- **Luke 2:8-15** ("... Do not be afraid ... I am bringing you good news of great joy for all the people. ...")
- **Isaiah 61:1-3** ("... [The LORD] has sent me to bring good news to the oppressed, to bind up the brokenhearted, to proclaim liberty to the captives, and release to the prisoners. ...")
- **John 3:17** ("God did not send the Son into the world to condemn the world, but in order that the world might be saved through him.")

After each Scripture is read, ask the youth first to identify the problem or bad news, then to indentify the good news that God provides as a remedy. Write these examples of bad and good news in the columns you created for the previous activity.

For example: In **Isaiah 61:1-3**, the bad news would include broken hearts, imprisonment, slavery and so on. The good news would include liberty, release, binding up, and so on.

As a class, come up with five to ten affirmations of the good news of the Christian faith by completing the sentence, "We believe the good news of the Christian faith is ..." Use the Scriptures above to guide your efforts. Record your affirmations next to your lists.

AND

Read a Creed, Write a Creed (13–17 minutes)

Provide copies of A Bad News/Good News Creed from page 49 and pens or pencils.

Invite the youth to read the creed, "Affirmation from Romans 8:35, 37-39" off of the handout from page 49.

Ask the youth to underline the bad news mentioned in this creed and to circle the good news. Then give individuals time to write their own creeds based on the model given on the handout. If time allows, ask for volunteers to read their creeds to the group.

i think i believe

Provide student journals and pens.

And Now, a Word from the "Doubt Side" (8–15 minutes)

Say: "Just like the characters in *Star Wars* wrestle with the 'dark side,' most Christians struggle with doubts about their faith and beliefs. We won't be able to address or answer all of those doubts right now, but we can at least become aware of the questions that many good Christians struggle to answer."

One at a time, ask a volunteer to read a question. Then discuss that question as a group before moving on to the next one:

- If God wants to bring us good news, why do bad things ever happen at all? Why doesn't God just eliminate all the bad news?
- How good is the news that "God is with us" in situations where our suffering continues? If God is "with us," shouldn't God be doing something?
- If Christians are called to spread the "good news," does that mean we all have to be optimists? When is it OK for Christians to be pessimists?

After discussing these questions, give the youth a few minutes to complete the activities, "Sometimes When I Doubt . . ." and "Things I Do Believe . . ." on pages 5–6 of the student journal.

lord, help me have faith

Pessimist's Prayer (2 minutes)

Have the youth gather in a circle and bow heads. Then read the following prayer aloud to the class:

Dear Lord,

I believe, but please help me and guide me when I have doubts.

Help me and inspire me, Lord, when all I can imagine is the problems, and not the solutions.

Help me and uplift me, Lord, when I feel down and depressed, when I am not even in the mood to listen to someone who is cheerful and optimistic.

Help me and bear with me, Lord, whenever I doubt you, or have doubts about my faith.

Help me and remind me, Lord, that you can accept me despite my deepest and most troubling questions.

Help me and teach me, Lord, to trust you, to believe in you, and to place my faith in you more and more each day.

Amen.

We Believe the Bible

Topic: For the Bible Tells Me So . . .

Scripture: Exodus 19:16—20:21; Ezekiel 1:28b—3:3; Luke 4:1-13, 16-21; 24:13-35; John 20:30-31; 2 Timothy 3:10-17; Revelation 22:18-19

Key Verse: "From childhood you have known the sacred writings that are able to instruct you for salvation through faith in Christ Jesus" (2 Timothy 3:15).

Take-Home Learning: God speaks to us through the Bible; it is the primary resource for Christians seeking understanding, inspiration, and guidance.

Younger Youth and the Topic

Many youth do not have established Bible reading habits. (Unless they have fallen into the habit of not reading it!) There are two significant barriers that keep youth, as well as adults, from reading the Bible regularly and making effective use of the Bible as a life resource. For one, many don't understand the Bible's function or where to start reading. Secondly, youth and adults alike often lack the self-discipline to develop a Bible reading routine.

Further, teens today have spent their young lives getting information in blurbs, graphics, and sound bytes. This is a visual, electronic, fast-paced generation, not one that gathers news from sitting down for a long read.

Today's youth can understand that while a scientific view of the world does not have to conflict with faith, it can conflict with a literal reading of the Bible. Where are dinosaurs mentioned? Were they on the ark? Why does the Creation story talk about a "firmament" and assume the world is flat when we know it is round? Some youth might dismiss the whole Bible as irrelevant because of such unreconciled questions and conflicts with their scientific view of the world.

What can you do? First, stress the many ways that the Bible can be a powerful resource, a wellspring of wisdom, and a source of comfort. Post Scripture verses around the room on posters, roleplay Bible stories, or set an important Scripture as the screen saver on your computer. Help youth deal honestly with their questions and doubts about the Bible, and push yourself to give these youth a solid overview of the Bible so they will not feel lost when they sit down to read Scripture.

Leader's Guide

The following definitions will be helpful for this session:

- **Biblical Inspiration**: the idea that God first spoke to the biblical writers, who were so moved by their encounters with God that they recorded what they had heard
- **Scripture**: any writing that a religion declares is sacred. For example, Muslims consider the Qu'ran "scripture"
- **The Word of God**: a theological term used by John to describe Jesus Christ. "Word" is the English translation of the Greek word, *logos*
- **God's word**: a promise made by God, a covenant

(continued on page 14)

More helpful definitions:

- **Inerrancy/Infallibility**: the belief that the Bible contains no embellishments, inconsistencies, or errors
- **Literal Interpretation**: the idea that every word in the Bible should be understood exactly as it is written
- **Exegesis**: methods of Biblical interpretation that seek deeper meaning by examining the historical context, looking for layers of meaning, considering the use of metaphors, exploring a book's form and structure, and so on

Spend time this week reflecting on some of your favorite Scriptures. Tell the youth about your experiences with the Bible and with these passages in particular.

Theology and the Topic

Biblical authority seems like a simple idea, but it is not. Why does the Bible have authority? What authority does it have? Over what or whom does it have authority? If persons claim to "believe the Bible," do they give equal weight to the commandments, "You shall not murder" (Exodus 20:13) and "If a woman will not veil herself, then she should cut off her hair" (1 Corinthians 11:6)? Both are in the Bible, yet many people use the authority of reason or church tradition to accept one commandment and not the other. Let's consider some of the terms and ideas central to understanding the authority of the Bible:

Books, documents, and laws receive their authority from a community. For example, the Christian community canonized the Old and New Testaments, giving them authority. However, the Catholic and Orthodox Christian communities include more books in their Old Testaments than Protestant Christians. Different Protestant communities place more or less emphasis on certain books of the Bible. The Jewish community canonized the TaNaKh (the books of the Protestant Old Testament in a slightly different order), giving it authority. Jews also recognize the authority of the Mishnah and the Talmud (books that interpret the TaNaKh). Thus most Jewish understandings of the authority of Scripture differ from most Christian understandings. Even though all of the various Christian and Jewish denominations have their roots in the ancient Hebrew Scriptures, they have come to understand the authority of Scripture in very different ways.

In John 1, the "Word of God" refers to Jesus Christ, the "Word of God" made flesh. Many Christians would say that Jesus and his teachings are really the ultimate authority. We come to know and obey this living Word primarily through the Bible, but also through our experience, our reasoning, and by the testimony of Christians through the centuries.

Some contend that the Bible is "infallible" or "inerrant," that it was directly communicated by God to the human writers with no mistakes or exaggerations of any kind. Others suggest the message of the Bible is "inspired" by God but was written by humans influenced by their cultural values and prone to the occasional mistake or inconsistency. Though the writing was guided by God, it was subject to human limitations. Still others consider the Bible an entirely human creation and critique the Bible from a modern scientific perspective. These persons are skeptical of supernatural miracles and certain theological assumptions. Then again, some Christians are concerned less with the nature and history of the Bible and more with the stories, lessons, and wisdom it provides.

You and the Scripture

This lesson is an opportunity for you to re-examine your own views about Scripture, and about the important role it can play in your life. To what extent has the Bible influenced your life so far or helped you grow as a Christian? If you sold your Bible in a rummage sale, how would not having a Bible change your life? Do you feel you make good use of your Bible? If not, how can you make your Bible a more important resource?

We Believe the Bible

Scripture: Exodus 19:16—20:21; Ezekiel 1:28b—3:3; Luke 4:1-13, 16-21; 24:13-35; John 20:30-31; 2 Timothy 3:10-17; Revelation 22:18-19

Take-Home Learning: God speaks to us through the Bible; it is the primary resource for Christians seeking understanding, inspiration, and guidance.

 indicates key activity. If time is limited, focus here.

activity	time	preparation	supplies
get ready			
Play Bible Games	7–10 minutes	Fill a bowl with small treats you have selected.	Bibles and a bowl of treats
some people say . . .			
The Bible's Authority	7–10 minutes	Duplicate the handout from page 50.	Handouts and pens or pencils.
OR			
Should You Throw Away an Old Bible?	8–10 minutes	No preparation	Student journals and pens
OR			
Invite a Guest	10–15 minutes	Invite members of the congregation to speak to your group or to provide lists of favorite Scriptures.	Members of the congregation
the bible says . . .			
(key activity) The "Whys" and "Hows" of the Bible	13–15 minutes	Write the eight Scripture passages from page 17 on a board or a large sheet of paper.	Bibles, a marker board or large sheet of paper, and markers
i think i believe			
(key activity) Here I Stand	4–6 minutes	Prepare the 5 sheets of paper according to the instructions on page 18.	5 sheets of paper prepared accordingly
lord, help me have faith			
(key activity) I Believe; Help My Unbelief!	7–12 minutes	Review Mark 9:14-29.	Student journals and pens

get ready

Provide Bibles and a bowl of treats such as candy or fruit.

To keep this game non-competitive, allow youth to assist one another. (Be prepared with plenty of treats.)

Feel free to create your own challenges if you'd like to spend more time on this activity.

some people say ...

Provide copies of the handout from page 50 and pens or pencils.

Provide student journals and pens.

Provide invited guests.

Leader's Guide

Play Bible Games (7–10 minutes)

Beforehand, prepare a bowl of candy, fruit, or other bite-size treats. As youth arrive, tell them they will be awarded with one treat every time they successfully complete one of the "Bible challenges" below.

- Close your Bible. Without looking at the table of contents or the thumb guides, open the Bible to the Book of Psalms. (For fun, see if anyone can open the Bible to Matthew or, for a real challenge, to Philemon.)
- Locate a quote from Jesus that isn't in one of the Gospels. (*Look to the opening chapters of Acts or Revelation.*)
- Locate a book of prophecy that begins with the letter "J." (*Jeremiah, Joel, or Jonah*)
- Find a word or name with the letters "aia" written in that order. (*Isaiah would be one.*)
- Read a proverb out loud. (*Award a bonus for a "proverb" outside of the Book of Proverbs.*)
- Find any quote from God.
- Find the Ten Commandments. (*Exodus 20; Deuteronomy 5*)
- Find a Bible somewhere in your church building with dust on it.
- Find a verse where Jesus mentions a camel. (*Matthew 19:24; Mark 10:25; Luke 18:25*)
- Find two verses that could offer guidance or comfort to a person struggling with a serious illness.
- Find a story of a miraculous healing.
- Find where it says, "For God so loved the world, that he gave his only Son, so that everyone who believes in him may not perish but may have eternal life." (*John 3:16*)

The Bible's Authority (7–10 minutes)

Distribute copies of the handout from page 50 and instruct the youth to complete the activities, "The Bible's Authority" and "Disagreement About the Bible." Be prepared to discuss questions and concerns.

OR

Should You Throw Away an Old Bible? (8–10 minutes)

Hand out student journals. Ask two volunteers to read the parts of Jim and Jane on pages 8–9. Discuss the questions that follow. (With a larger group, split into groups of four or five to discuss the questions.)

OR

Invite a Guest (10–15 minutes)

Ask one or more members of the congregation to come and talk about how they use the Bible, what wisdom they think it has to offer, and specific times God has spoken to them through the Bible.

Additionally (or instead), you may ask several church members to give you a list of one or more of their "favorite Scriptures." List each person's name on a sheet of paper followed by the Scriptures they suggest. Prepare copies of this list for your youth and suggest that they keep the list in their Bibles. (Be sure to make the list small enough to fit.)

Consider preparing a list of "favorite Scriptures" provided by various church members.

The "Whys" and "Hows" of the Bible (13–15 minutes)

Say: "The Bible is a collection of many different types of books, written over a long period of time by many different people. We're going to read a few Scriptures with two things in mind. First, we'll think about the type of Scripture. Is the passage a vision? a message? a parable? a story? a set of laws? and so on. Then we'll try to figure out the purpose of the passage. Was it written as a lesson? a word of advice? a warning? a message of inspiration? and so on."

Divide the youth into two groups. Assign each group one of the sets of four Scriptures below about the Bible and the power of the written word. For each passage, have the groups decide the type of Scripture and the purpose of the Scripture. While the youth are working, divide a board or large sheet of paper into three columns: One for the Scriptures themselves, one for the "types," and one for the "purposes." After the youth have had plenty of time to work, ask the groups to report the type and purpose they decided on for each Scripture. Write their answers on the board or large sheet of paper.

Group 1:

- **Exodus 19:16—20:21**
  Possible types: story; laws
  Possible purposes: to remember God's role in history; to offer moral guidance
- **Luke 4:1-13**
  Possible types: story; biography
  Possible purposes: to show Jesus' knowledge of the Scriptures; to show that even Jesus was tempted
- **Luke 24:13-35**
  Possible types: witness; story
  Possible purpose: to demonstrate that Jesus' resurrection was in accordance with the Scriptures
- **Revelation 22:18-19**
  Possible types: vision; witness
  Possible purposes: to offer a warning

Group 2:

- **Ezekiel 1:28b—3:3**
  Possible types: vision; witness
  Possible purposes: to show the power of God's word; to show how a prophet was inspired by God
- **Luke 4:16-21**
  Possible types: speech; story
  Possible purposes: to show Jesus' knowledge of the Scriptures; to show Jesus as the fulfillment of Scripture
- **John 20:30-31**
  Possible types: statement of purpose; conclusion
  Possible purpose: to explain why the book was written
- **2 Timothy 3:10-17**
  Possible types: letter; message
  Possible purposes: to instruct; to encourage; to proclaim that Scripture is inspired by God

Provide the five large sheets of paper prepared accordingly.

Here I Stand (4–6 minutes)

Write each of the five explanations (including the examples from Scripture) below on a separate large sheet of paper. Spread out these papers on the floor. Invite the youth to "take a stand" by standing next to the explanation that best describes how he or she understands the Bible. Invite volunteers to explain their choices. As volunteers offer their insight, allow youth to change their minds if they decide a different explanation is more appropriate.

- **The Bible as a mission statement that shapes our lives:** In Luke 4:16-21 Jesus expresses his mission by telling the crowd in Nazareth that his life is a fulfillment of Isaiah 61:1-3.
- **The Bible as a source of spiritual strength and guidance:** In Luke 4:1-13 Jesus turns to Scripture for support and guidance when confronted by temptation.
- **The Bible as a book of laws to follow:** In Exodus 19:16—20:21 God gives the Ten Commandments—the best known of the many laws given to God's people—to Moses and the Israelites.
- **The Bible as a witness for Jesus Christ:** In John 20:30-31 John states that the purpose of his book is to convince the reader that Jesus is the Messiah, the Son of God.
- **The Bible as a new way to understand life:** In Luke 24:13-35 the risen Christ interprets Scripture for two downcast disciples on the road to Emmaus, dramatically changing their perspectives on life.

lord, help me have faith

Provide student journals, and pens.

If some youth are uncomfortable holding up fingers, allow them to put their hands under a table, behind their backs, or in their pockets.

Consider keeping track of which statements are most fully believed or doubted. If time permits, discuss these statements.

I Believe; Help My Unbelief! (7–12 minutes)

Ask each youth to cut a sheet of paper into ten pieces. Read aloud Mark 9:14-29. Point out the disbelief of the people in verse 19. Also mention that the passage does not really say how this miracle affected the way the man, the disciples, or the people understood Jesus.

Say: "The man in this story is like all of us. He believes, but he also doubts. He wants to follow Jesus and believe in him, but he also struggles with what to believe about Jesus. The statement, 'I believe; Help my unbelief!' is memorable because the man is so honest about his lack of faith and his desire to grow in faith. Like most of us, this man is somewhere between a perfect believer and a complete doubter."

Turn to Appendix A on page 56. Tell the youth that you will read several statements of faith. Invite each youth to hold up a number of fingers to indicate how strongly he or she believes each statement—a *1* represents sincere doubt, while a *10* represents total belief. Stress that all answers are personal, but encourage youth to be honest with themselves. Mention that beliefs often develop over time—with God's guidance our faith will grow as we grow. After reading each statement, and allowing youth to reflect on their level of faith, invite the group to respond, "I believe Lord, but help me believe more."

End by asking youth to read page 10 and answer the questions on page 11 of the student journal. Close with prayer.

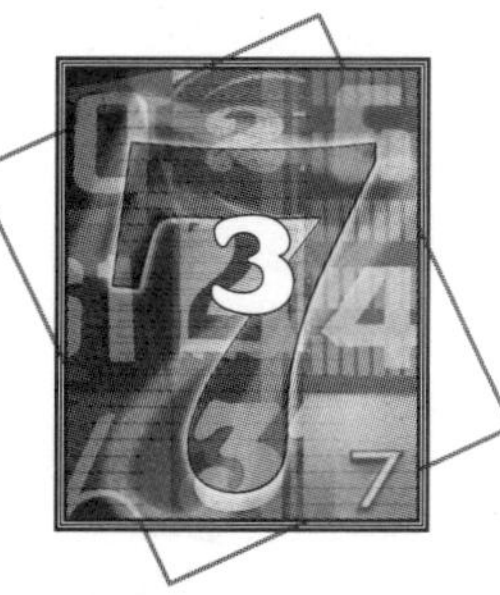

We Believe in God

Topic: Belief in One Triune God

Scriptures: Matthew 28:19-20; John 1:1-18; 14:8-20, 26; Acts 2:1-33; 2 Corinthians 13:13; Galatians 5:16-25; 1 Peter 1:2; 1 John 4:1-3

Key Verse: "Whoever has seen me has seen the Father . . . Believe me that I am in the Father and the Father is in me . . . I will ask the Father, and he will give you another Advocate, to be with you forever. This is the Spirit of truth whom the world cannot receive, because it neither sees him nor knows him. You know him, because he abides with you, and he will be in you" (John 14:9b, 11, 16-17).

Take-Home Learning: The Trinity is the church's way of expressing God's various roles and manifestations.

Younger Youth and the Topic

The doctrine of the Trinity is one of Christianity's most difficult theological concepts to understand, even for adults. The idea of "one God, three parts," is by nature philosophical and "heady." It cannot be acted out in a play like the story of the good Samaritan, nor does it appeal to the senses like the sight of Zacchaeus in the tree, the scent of the perfume poured on Jesus to anoint him, or the sound of the many voices shouting "Hosanna! Blessed is he who comes in the name of the Lord!"

Young adolescents are just beginning to have the mental capacity to deal with abstract ideas. These youth tend to learn actively by engaging their senses and dealing with concrete examples. Philosophical reflection is not their specialty. It may be difficult for these youth to grasp the concept of the Trinity, because it comes with no easy "handles."

One possible handle for youth is the idea of the Trinity as the network of relationships between the three persons, or manifestations, of God. Youth can identify with the relationship between a parent and a child, for example. Through the centuries the Trinity has been an important way for the church to describe God's many roles. Having even an elementary understanding of this mysterious doctrine enriches all biblical stories and events and will help youth grow in their understandings of God.

Theology and the Topic

In spite of the fact that the doctrine of the Trinity is central to Christian thought, the word *trinity* never actually appears in Scripture, and there are

<u>**Trinity Symbols**</u>:

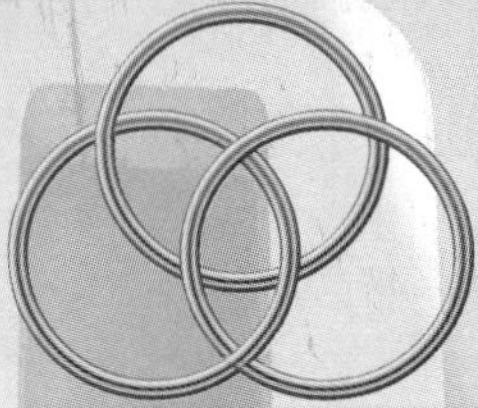

The three rings are locked together to form one structure. If any one ring is broken, the entire structure will fall apart.

The drops are of the same substance (water), and once commingled are indistinguishable from one another. However, each distinct drop clearly shows what it is made of. Likewise, each person of the Trinity reveals the same love, power, mercy, and so forth, that God is "made of."

Read through the following Scriptures, paying special attention to the descriptions of God as Father, Son, and Holy Spirit:

- **Matthew 28:19-20**
- **John 1:1-18**
- **John 14:8-20, 26**
- **Acts 2:1-33**
- **2 Corinthians 13:13**
- **Galatians 5:16-25**
- **1 Peter 1:2**
- **1 John 4:1-3**

only scarce references to the idea in the Bible. The doctrine developed through centuries of reflection, discussion, and disagreement. The Apostles' Creed, for example, began as a simple series of baptismal questions (based on Jesus' command in Matthew 28:19 to baptize "in the name of the Father and of the Son and of the Holy Spirit"). Therefore, candidates for baptism were asked, "Do you believe in God the Father?" ("Yes") "Do you believe in Jesus Christ, the Son?" ("Yes") "Do you believe in the Holy Spirit?" ("Yes") Over the centuries, the details in the Apostles' Creed were added for clarification, but it began as an affirmation of the belief in God as a triune being.

Ironically, to believe in God as the Trinity is to believe that there is only one God. Some saw Jesus as a challenge to this fundamental belief. As the "divine Son of God," Jesus potentially represented a second god! After all, he was divine, and he prayed to God as a father, as a separate being. To complicate matters, Jesus sent the Holy Spirit, yet another person or manifestation of God that appeared to be separate from God the Creator or God the Son. The Trinity is the church's way of affirming both the unity of God and the three experienced persons, expressions, roles, or manifestations of God.

Over the centuries the church considered some ideas about the Trinity heretical, such as the idea that Jesus was not really divine. So even though, as Christians, we affirm a sense of mystery about God, we do hold to some fundamental truths. We cannot fully know or understand God, yet God has made God's self known to us as creator (God the Father or parent), redeemer (God the Son or Christ), and sustainer (God the Holy Spirit or advocate).

You and the Scripture

When you agreed to teach these youth, you probably did not think you would be asked to describe God in detail, in one lesson, to a group of sleepy junior highs! This is your job, but it is a job that is too hard for anyone to do completely. In fact, seminary professors with Ph.D.s in theology write whole books about the doctrine of the Trinity. They eloquently analyze the history of doctrine, throw around Greek and Hebrew words, and crank out hundreds of pages on subtopics like "Sabellianism," "Arianism," and "Homoousion." Yet a realist might legitimately suspect that the entire scholarly work, however thick and difficult to read, is still merely a clay pot yakking about the potter!

Once you admit that nobody can really adequately describe God then you have taken the first step of faith. God is so vast, so awesome, so beyond our understanding that we could never do God justice with human words. We are the clay. God is the potter.

Still, as the clay, we feel God's hands at work in our lives. We can feel the love of God, and we are shaped by God's divine plan. Our feeble attempts to describe God, whether as the Holy Trinity or simply as awesome, will never be adequate. We must remember that the word *theology* literally means "(mere) words about God." So when all the words have been said—when the clay quiets down for a moment—remember that you are still in the hands of the potter.

We Believe in God

Scripture: Matthew 28:19-20; John 1:1-18; 14:8-20, 26; Acts 2:1-33; 2 Corinthians 13:13; Galatians 5:16-25; 1 Peter 1:2; 1 John 4:1-3

Take-Home Learning: The Trinity is the church's way of expressing God's various roles and manifestations.

 indicates key activity. If time is limited, focus here.

activity	time	preparation	supplies
get ready			
Tell a Riddle	3–5 minutes	No preparation	No supplies
some people say ...			
 Define and Discover Symbols of Trinity	15–20 minutes	Obtain Bible and theological reference books, and copies of creeds and denominational statements of faith.	Appropriate resources and reference materials, a marker board or large sheet of paper, and markers
the bible says ...			
 Match Scriptures with the Creeds	15–20 minutes	Duplicate the Match 'em Up! handout from page 51.	Bibles, handouts, and pens or pencils.
i think i believe			
 Make a Poster Series	15–20 minutes	Review instructions on pages 23–24 to consider options and alternatives.	Three poster boards, markers, and various art supplies
lord, help me have faith			
Lord, Is It a Sin to Doubt You?	10 minutes	Review the questions on page 24.	Student journals and pens.

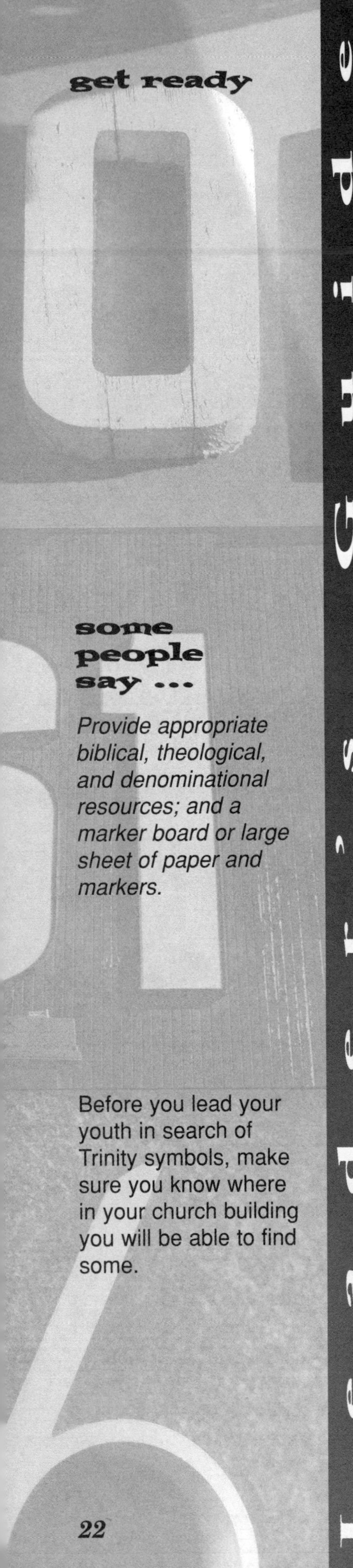

get ready

some people say ...

Provide appropriate biblical, theological, and denominational resources; and a marker board or large sheet of paper and markers.

Before you lead your youth in search of Trinity symbols, make sure you know where in your church building you will be able to find some.

Tell a Riddle (3–5 minutes)

Tell the class the following riddle: "Two fathers went fishing in a boat. Each father took one son with him. The fishing was just average; every person in the boat caught exactly one fish. But at the end of that day, only three fish had been caught. How could that be?" (*The boat contained three people, a grandfather, his son, and his grandson. Two of them were fathers, and two of them were sons. The "man in the middle" played two roles—father and son.*)

Give the youth a few minutes to think through the riddle before revealing the solution. Make an analogy to the idea of the Trinity. Say: "Just like one man in the boat was both a father and a son, each of you plays multiple roles in your life. To a friend, you are a friend. To your parents, you are their son or daughter. To your teachers, you are their student. Therefore, the same person can be a friend, a son or daughter, and a student. In the same way, we believe there is only one God, and yet we experience God as the creator of all that is, as Jesus Christ our Savior, and as the Holy Spirit who is the continuing presence of God with us."

Define and Discover Symbols of Trinity (15–20 minutes)

Beforehand, obtain a dictionary, a Bible dictionary or dictionary of theological terms, and a concordance. Also research and provide creeds and statements of faith from your denomination concerning the Trinity.

Say: "As a group, we're going to work together to write a definition of 'Trinity,' using information gathered from a variety of sources." Give the youth about five minutes to read through the resources you have provided. ("Trinity" should not be found in a concordance; when youth cannot find it listed, explain that the word *trinity* is not found in the Bible.)

Ask: "What words and phrases should we include in our definition of 'Trinity?'" Record the youths' answers on a marker board or a large sheet of paper. Then, as a group, come up with a common definition using some of these words and phrases.

Once you are comfortable with your definition, lead the youth on tour of your church building in search of symbols of the Trinity. Check the sanctuary, banners, floors, clerical stoles, pulpits, stained glass windows, and so on. The most common symbol is three interlocking circles, though you might find three drops of water coming out of a scallop shell near a baptismal font. If you don't know of any Trinity symbols in your church, invite the youth to look up Christian symbols for the Trinity in a book or on the Internet. (There might even be a church named "Trinity" in your community that uses one of these symbols on their church sign or in its Yellow Pages ad!)

Match Scriptures with the Creeds (15–20 minutes)

Hand out copies of the Match 'em Up! handout from page 51. Ask for volunteers to read each of the Scriptures below aloud to the group. After each one is read, look at the statements from creeds listed on the handout. As a group, decide which statements could be drawn from the Scripture that was read. Try to find as many matches as possible for each Scripture. This will probably mean linking several of the creedal statements to more than one Scripture. (Part of each Scripture has been provided for your benefit.)

- **Matthew 28:19-20** ("Go therefore and make disciples of all nations, baptizing them in the name of the Father and of the Son and of the Holy Spirit . . .")
- **John 1:1-18** ("In the beginning was the Word and the Word was with God and the Word was God. . . . He was in the world and the world came into being through him . . .")
- **John 14:8-20, 26** ("Whoever has seen me has seen the Father. . . . I will ask the Father, and he will give you another Advocate, to be with you forever.")
- **Acts 2:1-33** ("All of them were filled with the Holy Spirit and began to speak in other languages, as the Spirit gave them ability. . . .")
- **2 Corinthians 13:13** ("The grace of the Lord Jesus Christ, the love of God, and the communion of the Holy Spirit be with all of you.")
- **Galatians 5:16-25** ("Live by the Spirit, I say, and do not gratify the desires of the flesh. . . .")
- **1 Peter 1:1b-2** ("To the exiles . . . who have been chosen and destined by God the Father and sanctified by the Spirit to be obedient to Jesus Christ . . .")
- **1 John 4:1-3** ("By this you know the Spirit of God: every spirit that confesses that Jesus Christ has come in the flesh is from God . . .")

Then hand out student journals and allow youth time to complete "My Creed" on pages 12–13.

the bible says . . .

Provide Bibles, student journals, copies of the Match 'em Up! handout from page 51, and pens.

(Ask for volunteers instead of selecting youth to read out loud. Some youth are shy, in a bad mood, or just prefer to listen to others. One widely reported survey found that fear of reading in public ranked as high as fear of death for many people! A youth should not avoid Sunday school because he or she fears embarrassment because of his or her poor reading skills.)

Make a Poster Series (15–25 minutes)

Prepare three poster boards according to the directions below and hang them next to one another in your meeting space.

Write, "We believe in one God," in bold letters stretching across all three poster boards. Directly below this phrase, in a different color and in smaller letters, write "Father" on the left poster, "Son" on the middle poster, and "Holy Spirit" on the right poster.

Invite the youth to write words or statements on the appropriate poster that apply to each of the three persons of God. Some words or phrases might apply to all three persons; thus youth may write the same word or phrase on all three posters. Other words or phrases may be unique to one person. To make this activity more challenging, use one of the following design methods: Cut out individual newspaper letters to construct the words and phrases; create crossword puzzle-style

i think i believe

Provide three poster boards, markers, and various art supplies.

Instead of making three posters to put up in your room, you might consider making larger, more permanent cloth banners that you could display for others in the church building.

Invite youth to display these symbols on the posters. Some symbols might work on more than one poster.

lord, help me have faith

Provide student journals and pens.

interlocking words on each banner; or make a continuous line of words that form a spiral. Allow youth to be creative!

Alternatively, you could ask the youth to create symbols for the different roles of the Trinity. For example, they might make a picture of the earth or a flower to symbolize God as the creator, a picture of a shoulder with a hand on it to symbolize God as our guide, a picture of the cross to symbolize God our redeemer, and so on.

Lord, Is It a Sin to Doubt You? (Somebody Else Wants to Know.) (10 minutes)

Hand out student journals and ask youth to turn to "Is It a Sin to Doubt?" on pages 14–15. Instruct them to answer the first question on page 14 (question #1 below). Encourage youth to discuss their ideas and answers.

1. In your opinion, which of the following seem like sins? Why?

- **a.** Doubting or struggling with what to believe
- **b.** Believing in God, but disobeying God anyway
- **c.** Wondering whether God is listening when you pray
- **d.** Deciding to forget God and just doing whatever feels good
- **e.** Feeling torn between what you learn in science class and what you learn from the Bible in Sunday school and church
- **f.** Questioning why a loved one died even though you prayed for him or her to live
- **g.** Turning off a TV preacher who tells you how much money God wants you to send his TV show
- **h.** Attending church without really thinking about what you believe or what good it does to go to church
- **i.** Wondering why, if there really is a God, terrible things happen in the world

Say: "If you ever have doubts about God, then you are in the company of some of history's greatest and most faithful Christians! Doubts are a way of questioning what is real, and of discovering what you truly believe. In other words, doubts are often an important part of being a believer. The struggle of doubting can strengthen a person's faith, much like going through fire can purify metal.

"Even Jesus had questions about what direction his ministry should take. He questioned whether to go to Jerusalem to die on the cross both before the transfiguration and again in the Garden of Gethsemane. On the cross, he asked, 'My God, my God, why have you forsaken me?' Yet even as Jesus was questioning God, he was talking to God about his questions. In this way, doubts are an inner conversation with God."

Instruct youth to answer questions #2 and #3 on page 15 of their student journals. Then close with prayer.

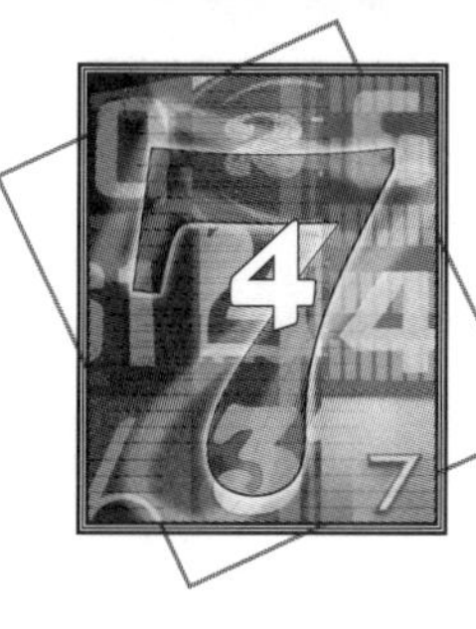

We Believe in Jesus Christ

Topic: Who Is Jesus to You?

Scripture: Matthew 16:13-20; John 1:1-18; 20:24-31; Acts 2:22-24, 32-42; Romans 5:6-10; Philippians 2:5-11; Colossians 1:15-20

Key Verse: "He said to them, 'But who do you say I am?' Simon Peter answered, 'You are the Messiah, the Son of the living God'" (Matthew 16:15-16).

Take-Home Learning: Many people wondered who Jesus really was. As Christians we must decide who Jesus is for us.

Younger Youth and the Topic

Youth are all over the map when it comes to knowing Jesus and knowing about Jesus. Some youth have a deep, personal faith and feel personally motivated to read the Scriptures. (A few even carry the Bible with them at school so they can do extra reading.) Others would be hesitant if you asked them whether they could read about Jesus in the Old Testament or New Testament. Still others get their knowledge of Jesus entirely from documentaries on cable television.

Most youth who have attended church with some regularity know the basics of Jesus' life—that he was born, was baptized, died, rose from the dead, ascended into heaven, and so on. However, even youth who have sat through several years of Sunday school classes may never have pieced together Jesus' life as one coherent story. This is because many children and younger youth appropriately learn about Jesus' life through snippets—individual stories and parables often taught one at a time, mixed in with stories of Moses, Paul, and others. This session presents an opportunity to help youth consolidate what they already know about Jesus into one overall story.

It is also important for youth to move beyond knowing about Jesus simply as a historical person to knowing Jesus personally as their own Lord. Guide your youth by questioning them as Jesus questioned of Simon Peter, first asking "Who do people say that Jesus is?" then asking, "Who do YOU say that Jesus is?" The second question asks each youth to define his or her relationship with Christ. It is certainly not too early for youth to wrestle with their answer to this important question in a way that is appropriate to them.

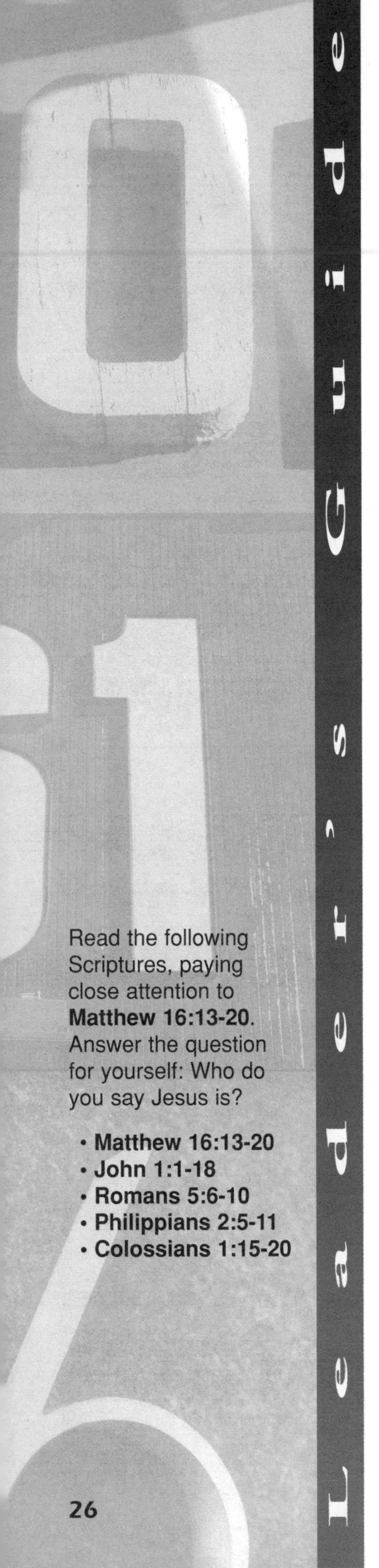

Read the following Scriptures, paying close attention to **Matthew 16:13-20**. Answer the question for yourself: Who do you say Jesus is?

- **Matthew 16:13-20**
- **John 1:1-18**
- **Romans 5:6-10**
- **Philippians 2:5-11**
- **Colossians 1:15-20**

Theology and the Topic

The person and nature of Jesus Christ is the most meaningful and complex topic in Christian theology. For now, let us divide the large topic of "Jesus Christ" into two subtopics commonly used by theologians: "The Person of Christ" and "The Work of Christ."

The Person of Christ refers to the physical and spiritual makeup of Jesus Christ. Remember that the authors of the Gospels believed Jesus was born of the Virgin Mary, and that his earthly father, Joseph, was not his biological father (even though the patriarchal genealogies in Matthew and Luke trace Jesus' lineage back to David through Joseph and not Mary). Jesus' father was God, at least in terms of determining his characteristics. Therefore, it has been a key Christian doctrine to say that Jesus was both 100 percent human and 100 percent divine. Mathematically it does not add up, but Christians long ago declared it a heresy to say that Jesus was half God and half human. If Jesus is to be our model, it is important that he was fully human—fully capable of experiencing temptation, pain, and all the things we do. On the other hand, Jesus clearly possessed all the loving and miraculous characteristics of God and even overcame death. He was "God in the flesh." So any attempt to shortchange either Jesus' humanity or divinity is to compromise something vital about the person of Jesus.

The Work of Christ is easier to understand. Jesus' single most important work was to give himself as a sacrifice for our sins. Though he struggled with his decision to make this ultimate sacrifice, he knew that his suffering would be temporary and its impact would be eternal. The work of Christ would also include Jesus' role as a healer, prophet, teacher, friend, and continuing example as our Lord, Teacher, and Redeemer.

You and the Scripture

After a major snowstorm recently swept through our region, my youngest son and I needed to walk out to the car. My son was not wearing boots, and he asked me if I would take the lead so that he could walk in my footsteps and not get so much snow in his shoes. When we were about half-way to our car, my son told me that the steps I was taking were too big for him and asked me to take smaller steps.

My son's experience following me is much like our experience following Jesus. Though we aim to follow in his footsteps, we sometimes feel like Jesus' steps are a little bigger than we can handle. It is a challenge to fit our walk to the Lord's. But when Jesus says to us, "Who do you say that I am?" we can answer by saying that he is the one leading, and we are the ones trying to follow.

The act of teaching these youth should push you to stretch your spiritual life and to grow, to strive to take bigger steps, steps that may be uncomfortable. Like the disciples, when you follow Jesus you are following in the footsteps of God.

We Believe in Jesus Christ

Scripture: Matthew 16:13-20; John 1:1-18; 20:24-31; Acts 2:22-24, 32-42; Romans 5:6-10; Philippians 2:5-11; Colossians 1:15-20

Take-Home Learning: Many people wondered who Jesus really was. As Christians we must decide who Jesus is for us.

 indicates key activity. If time is limited, focus here.

activity	time	preparation	supplies
get ready			
 Jesus' Life Timeline	10–15 minutes	Prepare index cards and create a line according to the instructions on page 28 and Appendix B on page 57.	Bibles, index cards, and masking tape OR a marker board or large sheet of paper and markers
some people say . . .			
 Consult the Creeds	10 minutes	Obtain statements about Jesus from various Christian creeds.	Statements, a marker board or large sheet of paper, and a marker
the bible says . . .			
Continue "Consult the Creeds"	13–15 minutes	Keep the lists made during the "Consult the Creeds" activity.	Bibles and the lists from the previous activity
AND			
 Who is Jesus to You?	15–20 minutes	Duplicate the Metaphors for Jesus handout from page 52.	Handouts and pens
i think i believe			
Pictures of Jesus	15–20 minutes	Gather different pictures of Jesus to supplement those in the student journal.	Student journals and various pictures of Jesus
lord, help me have faith			
Closing Worship	7–10 minutes	Review John 20:24-31.	Bibles, one candle for each youth, and matches

Jesus' Life Timeline (10–15 minutes)

get ready

Provide Bibles and index cards (or sticky notes) prepared accordingly. Also provide a marker board or large sheet of paper and markers or masking tape.

Allow youth to struggle with this exercise, to correct one another, and to check their answers with the Bible.

Before telling the story of Jesus, make any necessary corrections to the timeline.

Beforehand, write each statements from Appendix B on page 57 on a separate index card or sticky note. (Use a different color to indicate key events.) Mix up these cards and place them on a table. Then either draw a line with a marker across a marker board or large sheet of paper or make a line on the wall or the floor with masking tape.

As youth arrive, ask them to arrange the events of Jesus' life on the timeline. Instruct youth to put the cards in chronological order and to stick the cards (in order) to the timeline you've created. Hand out Bibles so the youth will have a reference. Tell the youth that some of the events are false and should not be included on the timeline.

Advise the youth to start by ordering the key events (such as birth, baptism, crucifixion, and so on) that you have marked. The other events should be arranged in relation to these key events.

When the correct cards have been placed in the correct order, tell the story of Jesus, leading the youth through one event at a time.

Consult the Creeds (10 minutes)

some people say ...

Provide statements concerning Jesus Christ from various Christian creeds, a marker board or large sheet of paper, and a marker.

Briefly explain to the youth that the church's doctrines or beliefs about Jesus can be divided into two categories: The Person of Christ (statements about who Jesus Christ was and is) and The Work of Christ (statements about the things that Jesus said or did).

Divide a marker board or large sheet of paper into two columns as shown below:

Who was Jesus Christ? (The Person of Christ)	What did Jesus Christ do? (The Work of Christ)

Invite the youth to look at statements about Jesus from various Christian creeds. As a group, decide which column is appropriate for each statement. When you are finished, review both lists to summarize the person and work of Christ.

Continue "Consult the Creeds" (13–15 minutes)

the bible says...

Provide Bibles and lists from the "Consult the Creeds" activity.

As a group, add one or more statements to your lists from the "Consult the Creeds" activity that summarize any of the following Scriptures:

- Matthew 16:13-20
- John 1:1-18
- Acts 2:22-24, 32-42
- Romans 5:6-10
- Philippians 2:5-11
- Colossians 1:15-20

AND

Who is Jesus to You? (10–15 minutes)

Distribute copies of the Metaphors for Jesus handout from page 52. Ask the youth to follow the instructions and complete the activity. Invite volunteers to tell how they answered the questions.

On a marker board or large sheet of paper, list the metaphors for Jesus found in the verses from John listed on the handout. Ask the students what each one means, and how each metaphor describes Jesus.

Then ask the youth to take a second look at the metaphors for Jesus found in John's Gospel and the additional metaphors on the handout. Ask: "Which of these metaphors is most meaningful to you? Why?"

Provide Bibles, copies of the Metaphors for Jesus handout from page 52, and pens.

Pictures of Jesus (10–15 minutes)

Invite youth to look at the various pictures of Jesus printed on pages 16–17 of the student journal. If you have access to other art prints of Jesus, look at some of those as well. Ask:

- Which of these pictures is most like how you picture Jesus?
- Do you think you would have chosen a different picture if you had been born or raised in a different culture? Why?
- What personality traits come to mind as you look at these pictures?
- Why do you think these artists chose certain poses for Jesus? What might the artist be saying about Jesus through his pose?
- If you could make one of these pictures of Jesus come to life and become your lifelong friend, which picture would you chose? Why?
- What events in Jesus' life are not being represented by these pictures? What events would you like to add?

Say: "Imagine that the pastor asked *you* to paint a picture for the sanctuary that would show what Jesus was really like." Ask:

- What would your picture look like?
- Would anyone be in the picture with Jesus?
- What would Jesus be doing? Would he have a certain pose or facial expression?
- What colors would you use?

Say: "Imagine that Jesus was in town for one week, and you had been asked to photograph the event for a national news magazine that needs one 'perfect picture' for its cover." Ask:

- What is your idea of the perfect picture of Jesus?
- Where might Jesus be in your picture?
- With whom might Jesus be talking or spending time?
- What might Jesus be doing?

Then allow youth time to answer the questions under "What's Jesus Really Like?" on pages 18–19 of the student journal.

i think i believe

Provide student journals, various pictures of Jesus and (if any are available).

If time permits, provide paper and pencils, colored pencils, or markers and allow youth to create their own pictures of Jesus. Encourage them to be thoughtful and creative. Display these in your meeting space.

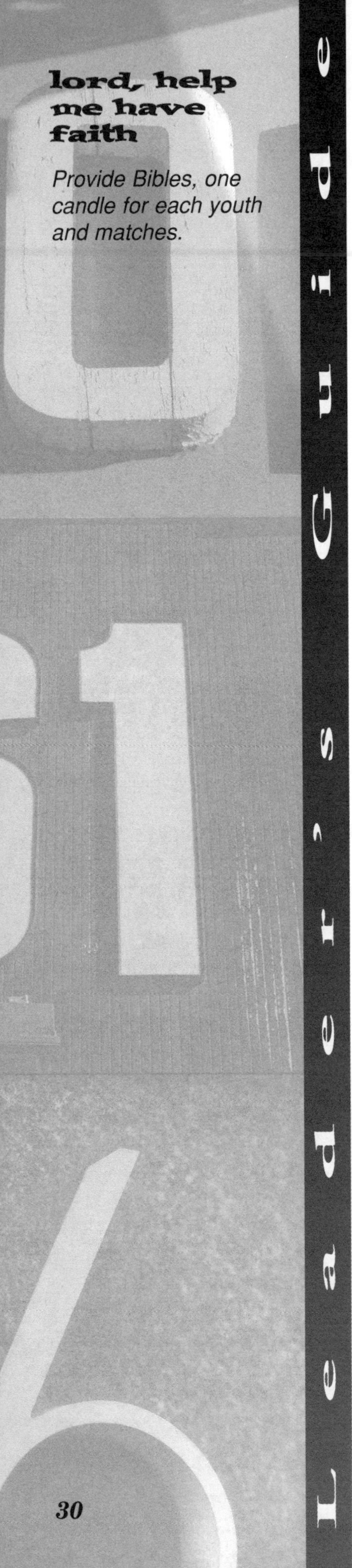

lord, help me have faith
Provide Bibles, one candle for each youth and matches.
Leader's Guide

Closing Worship (7–10 minutes)

Say: "The story of 'Doubting Thomas' takes place after Jesus' resurrection. Thomas is a disciple who refuses to believe that Jesus has been raised from the dead until he had proof." Ask a volunteer to read John 20:24-25, the first part of the story of "Doubting Thomas."

Say: "A week later, Jesus appears to Thomas and shows Thomas his wounds as proof of his resurrection. Which of the following statements would you expect Jesus to say to Thomas?"

- I can never forgive you for wanting proof! It just proves that you are not really one of my followers.
- I'll forgive you . . . this time. Don't let it happen again.
- Peace be with you, Thomas. You are forgiven.

Have a volunteer continue the story by reading John 20:26-29. Then say: "Notice how Jesus helps Thomas believe when he doubts instead of condemning Thomas for his doubts. Keep in mind how Thomas has struggled with his doubts for an entire week before he gets proof of Jesus' resurrection when he actually sees Jesus face to face."

Ask a volunteer to continue by reading John 20:30-31. Say: "Throughout his Gospel John raises the question, 'Who is Jesus?' John shows us how many different people answer this question—Jesus is a prophet, he is the Messiah, he is the light of the world, he is the resurrection and the life. Even 'Doubting Thomas,' after getting proof, calls Jesus his Lord and his God. Still, the real question is, 'Who Jesus is to *you*?' Like John wrote, all of this has been written to help you believe in Jesus, so that you can have faith, and through your faith in Jesus you may have life."

Offer a closing prayer. If you feel comfortable, invite youth to take a new step of faith in Christ. If appropriate, use a symbol such as one candle for each youth. Allow each youth to light his or her candle before the prayer to symbolize how God will increasingly take away the darkness of doubt and replace it with the light and joy of belief in Jesus Christ.

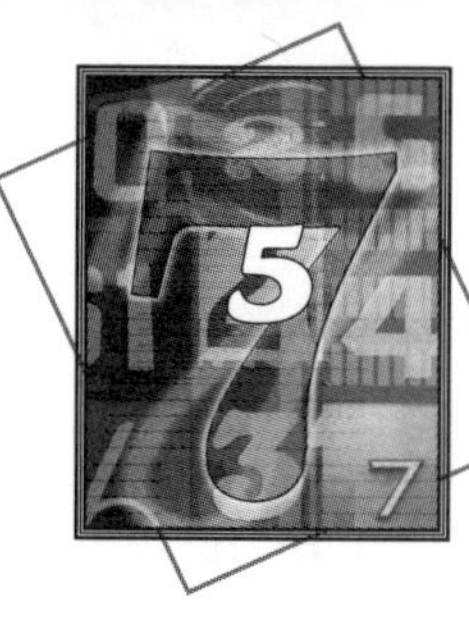

We Believe in the Church

Topic: The Church Is the Body of Christ

Scripture: Acts 2:37-47; 1 Corinthians 12:12-27; Ephesians 4:1-6, 11-16

Key Verse: "Now you are the body of Christ and individually members of it" (1 Corinthians 12:27).

Take-Home Learning: Through the life and work of the church, God accomplishes God's will on earth.

Younger Youth and the Topic

One person filled out a job application. Where the form asked for "church preference," the person wrote "red brick." This view may not be far from where some youth are! Asked what a church is, many youth will say it's a building. (Many adults will, too.) How many "church histories" are simply a record of the various buildings and new additions to the buildings made by that congregation?

Many others think of the church as a congregation—a group of people tied to a certain location and denomination who come together on Sundays, maybe Wednesdays, worship, sing, and share prayer requests. For some of these youth, going to church is just part of their social lives.

As youth grow in their ability to think abstractly, they also need to learn and discover that the church is not just another social group like a club or a clique. Further, the social groups that exist at school should not be carried over into the church. On the contrary, youth can be challenged to let the concept of church as a loving, accepting community help them break down the cliques at school.

Unfortunately, the church is often not a youth's first priority. Confirmation classes, for example, are squeezed amongst their participants' hectic schedules of school and community activities. Volleyball and wrestling practices are "required" by the coach, but what would happen if a pastor tried to "require" Sunday school or youth group attendance? This session is a good opportunity to ask youth what claim the church has on their lives.

Leader's Guide

Theology and the Topic

Ekklesia is the Greek word for "church" used in the New Testament. Thus "ecclesiology" is the study of the formal doctrine of the church. *Ekklesia* referred to the community of believers whose formation and growth is especially detailed in the Book of Acts. The Christian church was born on Pentecost (see Acts 2) when the Holy Spirit descended on the gathered believers following Jesus' ascent into heaven. Thus, the church could be defined today as the group of believers who, inspired by the Holy Spirit, continue the life, teaching, and work of Christ in the world. The church has been around for nearly 2000 years and will continue into eternity.

The church is a community of worship, mutual support, witness, evangelism, spiritual formation, and service, among others. The church is also responsible for administering rituals and sacraments. Baptism is a "rite of entry" into the church, and the Communion ritual defines the gathered people as the "body of Christ, redeemed by his blood."

The authority of the church has been an important issue from the very beginning when the Twelve assumed leadership roles (with Peter as the head of the entire operation), even though there were soon thousands of other believers. Today nearly all denominations have some sort of hierarchy, ordaining certain persons as bishops, elders, deacons, presbyters, and so on. The authority of the church is not merely a human invention; Jesus selected Peter as the original leader of the church (Matthew 16:18). The authority of all church leaders is grounded in the belief that they should be persons of good character who have a mature faith and who are called and inspired by God to lead—not just persons interested in a career.

You and the Scripture

Read the following Scriptures keeping in mind that you are part of the body of Christ. Pray about what you can do to strengthen this body and its work here on earth.

- **Acts 2:37-47**
- **1 Corinthians 12:12-27**
- **Ephesians 4:1-6; 11-16**

Chances are, you have been a member of the church (not necessarily your local church, but the church in general) longer than the youth with whom you are working. What changes have you seen the church undergo over the years? How do you feel about the state of the church today in our society? What changes would you like to see in the future? How can you play a constructive role in bringing those changes about?

There is a saying, "If you want your church to be a friendly, caring place, then be a friendly, caring member." One single member of the church can significantly affect (for better or worse) how well the church serves as a witness to others. Working with these youth is a great way to strengthen the church, because the church is a community of people, some of whom will be looking to you for guidance as you teach this session. So may God strengthen you through the church, and may God strengthen the church through you!

We Believe in the Church

Scripture: Acts 2:37-47; 1 Corinthians 12:12-27; Ephesians 4:1-6, 11-16

Take-Home Learning: Through the life and work of the church, God accomplishes God's will on earth.

 indicates key activity. If time is limited, focus here.

activity	time	preparation	supplies
get ready			
What Is the Church? Survey	10–20 minutes	If you have Internet access, try to locate an Internet directory of churches in your area.	Paper, pens or pencils, phone books, newspapers, and an Internet-ready computer (optional)
some people say . . .			
 Balloon Creeds	12–18 minutes	Obtain two balloons for each youth. Duplicate The Church in the Creeds handout from page 53.	Handouts, balloons, string, and markers (student journals, sips of paper, and pens are optional)
AND			
Interview a Guest	10–15 minutes	Arrange for a pastor or another church leader to speak to your group.	The speaker and a list of questions for the speaker
the bible says . . .			
 Top Ten Purposes of the Church	12–16 minutes	Review the Scriptures on page 35.	Bibles, a marker board or large sheet of paper, markers, student journals and pens
i think i believe			
Make a Paper Chain	9–16 minutes	Cut out three red and three green strips of construction paper for each youth.	Strips of red and green construction paper, tape or a stapler, and markers
lord, help me have faith			
 Explore "We Are the Church"	10–15 minutes	Obtain hymnals or songbooks that include the song "We Are the Church."	Hymnals or songbooks, paper, and pens or pencils (a guitar or piano is optional)

get ready

Provide paper, pens or pencils, phone books, the religion page of a recent newspaper, and a computer with Internet access (optional).

Consider writing the instructions to the various assignments on index cards, so the youth will better remember what they are supposed to do.

What Is the Church? Survey (10–20 minutes)

Ask the first few youth who arrive if they would be willing to conduct a quick survey in your church while you wait for the others to arrive. Give each of these youth a sheet or pad of paper and a pen or pencil and instruct them to spend between five and ten minutes asking as many people as possible the following two simple questions:

- What is the church?
- What is the purpose of the church?

Allow youth to walk up and down hallways, to visit gathering places in the church, or to stop into other classes that are waiting for people to arrive. Since entire books could be written in response to either of these questions, tell the youth to ask for short answers.

If you have Internet access, arrange for the next few youth who arrive to look for purpose or mission statements on various church Websites. Ask these youth to print any statements they find. (Beforehand, try to locate an Internet directory of churches to use as a starting point.) Instruct the youth to summarize each purpose or mission statement with a single phrase. (For example: to win disciples, to teach the Bible, to raise funds and sponsor missionaries, to feed the hungry, to provide a house of worship, and so on.)

As more youth arrive, instruct some to look through your local phone book and count the number of churches listed. Ask these youth to pay special attention to the church advertisements and to think about what each ad says about a church's purpose or mission.

Instruct other youth to scan the religion page or section from a recent newspaper. Have these youth pretend they know nothing about the church, except what they have read in the paper. Ask these youth to write a description and purpose of the church based on the ads and articles in the paper alone.

After five or ten minutes, gather the youth back together and ask them to report what they learned about the church and its mission.

some people say ...

Provide copies of The Church in the Creeds handout from page 53, balloons, strings, and markers.

Balloon Creeds (12–18 minutes)

Beforehand, obtain enough solid-colored balloons so that each student can have at least two. Make sure the balloons are at least a foot tall and inflate these balloons beforehand, preferably with helium.

Distribute The Church in the Creeds handout from page 53 and ask the youth to look at the various affirmations of faith. (You might, instead, provide your church's doctrinal statements.) Encourage youth to choose and write on the balloons one or more phrases about the church, such as, "we believe in the church" or, "those who are united to the living Lord" or, "for the purpose of worship and service."

(For more insight into what the church is and does, hand out student journals and ask youth to look at the "Vows of Membership" on pages 20–21.)

If you use helium balloons, check in advance with your pastor or worship committee to see if you can put them together and display them during the worship service. If you use regular balloons, hang the balloons from the walls or ceilings of your meeting space.

Alternatively, use uninflated balloons and have youth write phrases dealing with the church on slips of paper. Instruct them to insert each slip of paper in a balloon then to blow up the balloon. Ask each youth to select one balloon. Then gather the youth in a circle and have them bat their balloons around to one another. Allow this to continue for a few minutes. When you stop, make sure everyone ends up with one balloon. Then have everyone pop his or her balloon by sitting on it. One at a time, have each youth read the statement hidden inside the balloon she or he popped and guess which person selected that statement. If you have enough balloons and enough time, repeat the activity.

AND

Interview a Guest (10–15 minutes)

Invite your pastor or another church leader to speak to your group about the church. Ask the guest speaker to address the following questions:

- What is the purpose or mission of *the* church?
- What does *this* church do as a part of that mission? Whom does our church reach out to?
- How can individual members strengthen the work of the church?
- If you had to take three photographs to represent the life and work of the church, what would those photographs look like?
- How do this church's budget and spending reflect the goals and mission of the church? What changes might you make if you could?
- What skills and talents have members of this church shared that have strengthened this congregation? the church as a whole?

Top Ten Purposes of the Church (12–16 minutes)

Read aloud each of the following Scriptures one at a time, trying to glean ideas about the purpose and mission of the church:

- **Acts 2:40-47**
- **1 Corinthians 12:12-27**
- **Ephesians 4:1-4, 13-16**

Make a list of the ideas gleaned from the Scriptures (try to come up with at least ten) and rank the top ten in order of importance.

Student journals, slips of paper, and pens are optional.

When inviting a guest speaker, remember the following:

- Give plenty of advance notice
- Be clear about the topic and subject matter.
- Make sure you know enough about your guest to give him or her a proper introduction.

the bible says . . .

Provide Bibles, a marker board or large sheet of paper, markers, student journals, and pens.

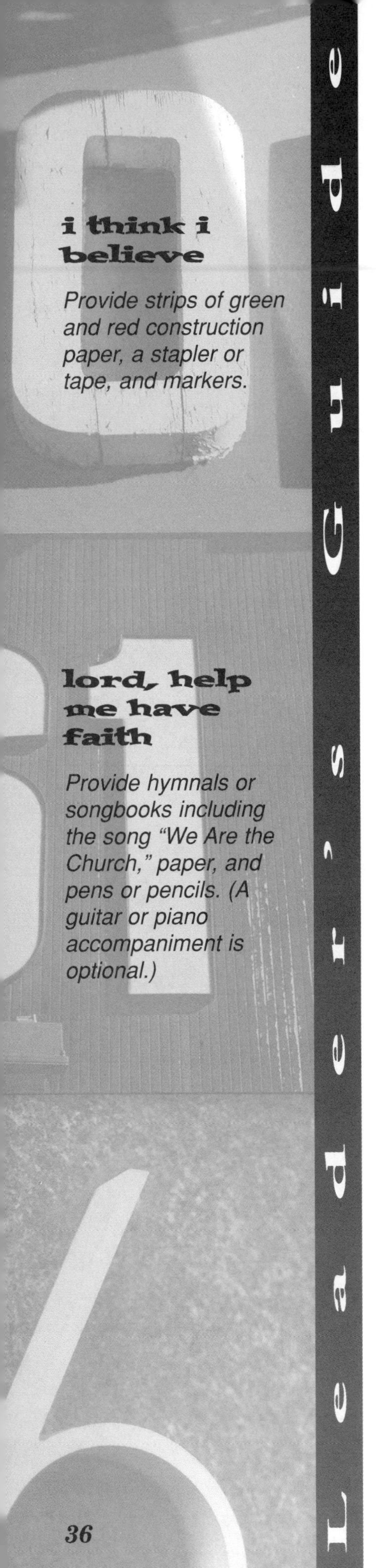

Hand out student journals and have students add their own answers to the "Twelve Silliest Reasons to Go to Church" on page 22. Then ask them to list some serious reasons for going to church on page 23.

i think i believe

Provide strips of green and red construction paper, a stapler or tape, and markers.

Make a Paper Chain (9–16 minutes)

Beforehand, cut out strips of red and green construction paper for a paper chain. Make sure there are a few strips of each color for each youth. Have the youth write on the red strips some of their beliefs about the purpose and mission of the church. On the green strips, have them write the names of the church's youth, adults who work with the youth, and youth they know from other churches. The put the chain together, with tape or a stapler, alternating green and red links.

Display the chain in your meeting space or elsewhere in the church. Say: "Our beliefs link us together. As each link plays a vital role in holding the chain together, each of us plays a vital role in the body of Christ. The Scripture tells us that in the church, though we are many individuals, we are all linked together as the one body of Jesus Christ."

lord, help me have faith

Provide hymnals or songbooks including the song "We Are the Church," paper, and pens or pencils. (A guitar or piano accompaniment is optional.)

 Explore "We Are the Church" (10–15 minutes)

Provide hymnals or songbooks and have youth look at the song, "We Are the Church." Divide the class into two groups. Ask one group to come up with hand motions to go along with the song. Instruct the second group to do a "reverse paraphrase" of the song by putting into their own words a song with the opposite meaning. (For example, "I'm not the church, you're not the church, we aren't the church," and so on.) Give the groups time to work then ask a volunteer from the second group to read the reverse paraphrase. Ask:

- What doubts about the church were expressed by the reverse paraphrase?
- How else might some people doubt the church?
- What doubts about the purpose and mission of the church are expressed when someone says, "I can worship just as well on the golf course enjoying God's creation"?
- How would you respond to a person who quits believing in the church after getting to know some Christians who don't live up to what the church proclaims?
- What words of encouragement does this song offer to people who doubt the church? How do the words of this song reach out to people who don't know much about the church?

As a closing worship experience, ask the first group to teach the others the hand motions for "We Are the Church," and then sing it together.

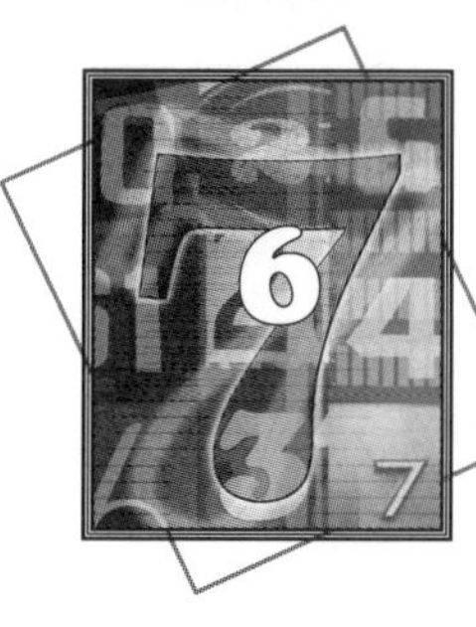

We Believe in Living This Life

Topic: Life in the Present

Scripture: Matthew 5:13-16; Luke 16:19-31; Ephesians 4:17-24; 5:1-2, 8-17; James 1:19-27; 1 John 4:7-21

Key Verse: "You were taught to put away your former way of life, your old self, corrupt and deluded by all its lusts, and to be renewed in the spirit of your minds, and to clothe yourselves with the new self, created according to the likeness of God in true righteousness and holiness" (Ephesians 4:22-24).

Take-Home Learning: Christians are called to a life of holiness and righteousness.

Younger Youth and the Topic

Many younger youth think that the main goal (or even the only goal) of being a Christian or accepting Jesus as one's Savior is to get to heaven. Because youth have a tendency to act as if they are immortal, death usually isn't the first thing on their minds. Many young adolescents can't imagine being twenty-five years old, let alone living in a nursing home! Issues like finishing the school year, finding a date for the dance, or making the team are more immediate concerns. Therefore, youth often struggle to connect their faith to their everyday lives. Some think to themselves, "Religion is about what happens after you die—right?"

Yes and no. Christians do believe in life everlasting, but Christianity also has a great deal to do with this life. Jesus dealt with issues of charity and justice in the world and commissioned his followers to do likewise. He also told his followers to live faithfully here and now. It is important for youth to know that, as followers of Jesus, they have certain responsibilities. Session Seven will explore life in the world to come, but this session will help youth see how their faith is relevant in the world in which they live.

Theology and the Topic

At one time Christians believed that the earth was the center of the entire universe, because earth is where the drama of God's salvation played out. Astronomers have demonstrated that we are more like a single, vulnerable speck spinning our way through the dangers of space in one galaxy of many billions. The church's teachings about this world have changed over the centuries, partly in response to these scientific discoveries.

Yet the most central and basic convictions have not changed and are reflected even in the most ancient Christian creeds. Some of our essential beliefs about life in this world include:

- We believe that this world was created by God but is temporary.
- We believe that God created the world to be perfect, but that human beings rebelled, by our own free will, introducing sin and death.
- We believe that since then God has been seeking ways to restore, redeem, and save us; therefore this world is caught in a struggle between the powers of evil and good.
- We believe God is still actively at work in this world.
- We believe that we should grow in faith in this life, serve other people, and seek to be more like Christ in our actions.
- We believe that no earthly kingdom can measure up to God's perfect ideal. Therefore Christians live in this world but are also citizens of God's perfect world. This makes us witnesses to a better way, like lights in the darkness.

You and the Scripture

Read the following Scriptures, focusing on Matthew 5:13-16:

- **Matthew 5:13-16**
- **Luke 16:19-31**
- **Ephesians 4:17-24**
- **Ephesians 5:1-2, 8-17**
- **James 1:19-27**
- **1 John 4:7-21**

Read the Scriptures for today, and then consider Christmas lights. Strands made up of many tiny bulbs can transform a tree or house into something bright and beautiful. If only one family on a block bothers to put lights in their bushes or railings, that home easily draws the attention of every driven and pedestrian who passes along that street.

In other words, it just takes a little bit of light to change things! Light draws attention to itself, particularly in a dark environment.

God created this world and declared it good, but now we live with terrorism, famine, poverty, disease, and war. We have polluted and altered so many habitats that many spectacular animals are going extinct. What is your assessment of the world we live in today?

- Has God given up on the world, or does God still have hope for God's creation?
- We all know there is plenty of darkness in our midst. Thus we must each decide how to respond. How can you, your church, and your youth, be lights for the world?
- What does it mean to believe in the life of this world?

We Believe in Living This Life

Scripture: Matthew 5:13-16; Luke 16:19-31; Ephesians 4:17-24; 5:1-2, 8-17; James 1:19-27; 1 John 4:7-21

Take-Home Learning: Christians are called to a life of holiness and righteousness.

 indicates key activity. If time is limited, focus here.

activity	time	preparation	supplies
get ready			
 Rank the World's Problems	7–10 minutes	Using masking tape, divide a tabletop into five sections, labeled accordingly. Prepare index cards accordingly.	Student journals, prepared pages and index cards, blank index cards, masking tape, and pens
some people say . . .			
Listen to "What a Wonderful World"	5–7 minutes	Obtain a recording of the song, "What a Wonderful World."	A recording of "What a Wonderful World," and a CD, cassette, or record player
AND			
 Color-Code the Creeds	8–10 minutes	Duplicate the Life in the Creeds handout from page 54.	Handouts, highlighters of various colors, a marker board or large sheet of paper, and pens or pencils
the bible says . . .			
 Compare the Scriptures to the Creeds	15–20 minutes	Keep the lists from Color-Code the Creeds.	Bibles, lists from Color-Code the Creeds, and markers
i think i believe			
Create a Bulletin Board Display	10–15 minutes	Keep the index cards from Rank the World's Problems; obtain a bulletin board.	A bulletin board, tacks, index cards from Rank the World's Problems, and markers of various colors
lord, help me have faith			
Create Your Own Creed	10–15 minutes	No preparation	Bibles, student journals, and pens

get ready

Provide student journals, prepared pages and index cards, blank index cards, and pens.

To save time you could provide blank index cards and have youth copy each problem from the student journal onto an index card as they are sorting the problems.

some people say ...

Provide a recording of the song, "What a Wonderful World," by any of the artists who have recorded it, and a CD or cassette player. (You might even need a record player!)

Be sure to read the note on permissions on page 42.

Leader's Guide

Rank the World's Problems (7–10 minutes)

Beforehand, use masking tape to divide a tabletop into five sections. Write each of the following statements on a sheet of paper and place each sheet of paper in one of the five sections:

- **Crisis**—Must solve! Threatens life on earth!!!
- **Urgent**—Spare no cost to find a solution!
- **Important**—Work on a solution, but take your time.
- **Trivial**—If you think of something, great; if not, it's no big deal.
- **Unimportant**—Don't waste your time worrying about it.

Using a black marker, write each of the "Problems of the World" listed on pages 24–25 of the Student Journal on a separate index card. Or make up some problems of your own.

Shuffle the cards thoroughly. As youth arrive, ask them to work together to decide in which category each problem belongs. Then have the youth sort the cards accordingly. If time allows, challenge the group to think of other problems for each category. Instruct youth to write these problems on index cards. Then have youth answer the questions on page 26 of their student journals ("For Your Extra Thought and Prayer") or ask:

- What other important problems would you still like to add?
- Which problems do you think God would find most urgent? Why? How might God have arranged these problems differently?
- Which problems do you think the church, or people of faith, should be working to solve? Why?
- If God agreed to solve any one problem of your choosing, which problem would you ask God to solve? Why?
- Which of these problems do you think will still be problems in heaven?

Listen to "What a Wonderful World" (5–7 minutes)

Play the song, "What a Wonderful World," and ask youth to listen carefully to the words. When the song has finished playing, take a poll. Ask:

- How many of you agree with the words of the song?
- How many of you disagree with the words of the song?

Ask volunteers to explain why they voted as they did. Then ask:

- How does the song make you feel about life? about the world?
- As Christians, how does our attitude toward the world in which we live affect our moods, our feelings, and the amount of effort we are willing to put into solve the world's problems?

Say: "There was a person who decided to eliminate the word 'problem' from her vocabulary. So whenever she heard or thought of the word 'problem,' she would substitute it with a word such as 'opportunity' or 'challenge.'" Ask:

- If you did this, how would it affect your actions and your view of the world?
- If the church as a whole did this, how would it affect our actions and our view of the world?

AND

Color-Code the Creeds (8–10 minutes)

Hand out copies of the Life in the Creeds handout from page 54 and ask each youth to choose two different colors of highlighters. Have them read the statements from the creeds listed on the handout. Then ask the youth to highlight in one color any parts of those statements dealing with what Christians believe God is doing, has done, or will do in this world. Ask youth to highlight in the other color any parts of those statements dealing with what Christians believe people are doing, have done, or should do in this world. If a word or phrase involves both God and people, youth may highlight that phrase with both colors.

Provide copies of the Life in the Creeds handout from page 54, highlighters of various colors, a marker board or large sheet of paper, and markers.

As a group, make two lists on a marker board or large sheet of paper. First list statements that speak of God's work in the world. Then list statements that speak of our work in the world. (Some statements will likely end up on both lists.)

Consider providing your church's statements of faith as well.

Keep these lists handy for the next activity.

Compare the Scriptures to the Creeds (15–20 minutes)

the bible says ...

Provide Bibles, the lists from Color-Code the Creeds, and markers.

Divide the youth into five groups. Assign each group one of the following scriptures:

- **Matthew 5:13-16** ("You are the light of the world. . . .")
- **Luke 16:19-31** (The rich man and Lazarus)
- **Ephesians 4:17-24; 5:1-2** ("You were taught to put away your former way of life . . .")
- **Ephesians 5:8-17** ("Live as children of light . . .")
- **James 1:19-27** ("Be doers of the word, and not merely hearers . . .")
- **1 John 4:7-21** ("Let us love one another, because love is from God . . .")

Ask each small group to discuss the following questions:

- If you only read this particular Scripture, what would you think of God's role in the world? What would you think of the church's role in the world?
- How do your answers to the previous question compare with the lists we made after looking at the creeds? Should anything be added to our lists?

Have each group report its answers to the others. Add any additional statements to the lists from the previous activity.

i think i believe

Provide a bulletin board and tacks, index cards from Rank the World's Problems, and markers.

Create a Bulletin Board Display (10–15 minutes)

This activity requires a bulletin board. If you do not have a bulletin board in your meeting space, or if your bulletin board features a permanent display, bring a bulletin board that you could hang temporarily. Or, in place of a bulletin board and tacks, you could use a poster board and tape.

Redistribute the index cards from Rank the World's Problems to the youth. Instruct them to write an "I Believe" statement on each card, explaining how God and the church can work together toward a solution to the problem. For example, for the problem of "Homelessness in America," a youth may write, "I believe that God, working together with Christians and organizations such as Habitat for Humanity, can help find homes for the homeless."

Encourage students to decorate each card with bright colors. When a student finishes a card, have him or her post it on the bulletin board.

lord, help me have faith

Provide Bibles, student journals, and pens.

Create Your Own Creed (10–15 minutes)

Ask the youth to reread Matthew 28:16-17 as a group. Explain that this verse follows the Resurrection, and that even some people who had seen the risen Christ with their own eyes doubted his resurrection. Yet despite their doubts, they continued to worship God.

Say, "Courage is not the absence of fear. After all, there are some circumstances, like fighting in a war, when it would be almost impossible not to be afraid. Instead, courage means to act bravely and to do what you are supposed to do despite your fears. In the same way, faith is not the absence of doubt; instead, it is possible to have doubts, but to still worship and act in a faithful way. That is why some of the disciples still worshiped Jesus despite their doubts. Like Matthew says, 'When they saw him, they worshiped him; but some doubted' (28:17).

"Some of the world's problems are so overwhelming that we sometimes lose faith or hope and question why God would allow such things to happen. However, this should not prevent us from working together with God to solve these problems and to make the world a better place."

Hand out student journals and allow time for youth to complete "Create Your Own Creed" on page 27. As the closing act of worship, allow volunteers to read aloud their creeds to the group.

Notes on Song Listening

When you play music from a CD or cassette for a group of learners, you need to obtain a license. Two companies offer this service: Christian Copyright Licensing, Incorporated (CCLI)—800-234-2446—and LicenSing—800-328-0200. Both will provide an annual list of publishers for whom they administer copyrights. Check with your church to see if an umbrella license has already been obtained. Many denominations—through conferences, jurisdictions, dioceses, and other structures—secure licenses for their churches.

We Believe in Eternal Life

Topic: God's Final Triumph

Scripture: Matthew 19:16-30; 25:31-46; 1 Corinthians 13:8-13; Revelation 20:11-21:8

Key Verse: "He will wipe every from their eyes. Death will be no more; mourning and crying and pain will be no more, for the first things have passed away. And the one who was seated on the throne said, 'See, I am making all things new . . . I am the Alpha and the Omega, the beginning and the end" (Revelation 21:4-6).

Take-Home Learning: At the end of the story, God is going to win. That means that nothing bad or evil will last, and everything good and holy will go on forever. Through Christ, even sinners can receive salvation and eternal life, which is a life of perfect love, joy, and peace in God.

Younger Youth and the Topic

In school, youth follow a continual life pattern of studying for a test, taking a test, and then not knowing the outcome until the test is "judged." Once the teacher gives a verdict (a grade), a student is typically powerless to change his or her performance on that test.

As a result of living this way, heaven, hell, and eternal life are potentially unnerving topics for youth. Many youth may interpret the final judgment as the "final exam" and their grade (and eternal fate) as still undetermined. "How can I know I will get into heaven?" they might nervously ask themselves, frightened of the alternative.

Judgment is only one aspect of what Christians believe about life after death. We also believe that God's goodness, love, and presence are certain and consistent in this life, in death, and in life beyond death. We also believe in God's mercy, in the Resurrection, and in the persistence of hope. We believe that God will restore justice and all that is good. These aspects of the Christian faith can be comforting and reassuring for youth and adults alike.

Theology and the Topic

In Christian doctrine, the term for the study of the end times is *eschatology*. Like most other elements of Christian doctrine, believers are not in perfect agreement about the end of the world, the final judgment, or heaven and hell. Here are some things to keep in mind:

- One should make a distinction between the words "immortality" and "resurrection." Immortality is simply living forever without dying. Some Christians believe the body and soul are separate and that the body will die while the spirit is immortal and will live forever. Resurrection, on the other hand, is to restore to life something that has died. Some Christians believe that God will one day revive and restore the bodies and souls of those believers who have died.
- Many Christians believe Jesus will return to judge the world and initiate his Kingdom of God. Others think God will transform this world either over time through the work of the church or instantly in the future through one dramatic act. Still others think there is no hope for this world, and that God will judge it, destroy it, and create a new world that is perfect.

At any rate, we should focus our attention most on the example of Jesus. He resisted all efforts to figure out exactly when the Kingdom of God would become a reality. Over the centuries, many people have guessed when and how the end would come through their interpretations of Scripture, particularly the book of Revelation. If you are reading this, you know that, so far, no one has been right. Therefore, it is appropriate and important to undergird all talk about the future in a respectful cloak of mystery and to trust in God's goodness. We do not know all the details, but it is enough to know that the future is in God's hands, for God is good and will ultimately triumph.

You and the Scripture

Read the following Scriptures in preparation for this session:

- **Matthew 19:16-30**
- **Matthew 25:31-46**
- **1 Corinthians 13:8-13**
- **Revelation 20:11—21:8**

There are plenty of problems in the world that seem impossible to solve: war, hunger, homelessness, drugs, disease, domestic violence, and crime, are just a few. On an individual level we face additional problems with our families, our finances, our health, and so on.

Many Christians think that there are no problems that God cannot ultimately solve. Many believe that, no matter what, God will someday bring about a gloriously happy future.

This session entertains these thoughts. Could it really be that no matter how far our world falls behind, God will ultimately make the "last-second shot to win the game?" Wouldn't life be easier if we knew that to be true? Our faith does not ask these questions; it boldly declares that God will prevail!

What do you believe? If you can believe what the Christian faith proclaims, how will your beliefs influence your choices and your attitude toward life?

We Believe in Eternal Life

Scripture: Matthew 19:16-30; 25:31-46; 1 Corinthians 13:8-13; Revelation 20:11-21:8

Take-Home Learning: At the end of the story, God is going to win. That means that nothing bad or evil will last, and everything good and holy will go on forever. Through Christ, even sinners can receive salvation and eternal life, which is a life of perfect love, joy, and peace in God.

 indicates key activity. If time is limited, focus here.

activity	time	preparation	supplies
get ready			
Heaven Can Wait	10–15 minutes	Obtain a copy of *Heaven Can Wait* on VHS or DVD. Read the notes on page 48. Get permission from parents.	Movie on VHS or DVD and VCR or DVD player
some people say . . .			
 Make a Collage	14–18 minutes	Gather various newspapers and magazines. Duplicate Afterlife in the Creeds handout from page 55.	Poster board, newspapers, magazines, student journals, handouts, denominational resources,and song books
AND			
Do a Bible Survey	13–20 minutes	Review the Scriptures listed on page 46.	Bibles, student journals, pens, a marker board or large sheet of paper, and markers
look for life			
 Visions of Heaven	12–15 minutes	No preparation	Student journals and pens
go with god			
 Closing Worship	8–12 minutes	Obtain hymnals or song books featuring "Hymn of Promise."	Bibles, hymns or song books, and other worship supplies (optional)

get ready

Provide a copy of Heaven Can Wait *on VHS or DVD and a VCR or DVD player.*

Feel free to substitute a different movie that shows heaven from a Hollywood perspective.

some people say . . .

Provide poster board, newspapers and magazines, student journals, copies of the Afterlife in the Creeds handout from page 55, denominational resources, and hymnals or songbooks.

the bible says ...

Provide Bibles, student journals, pens, a marker board or large sheet of paper, and markers.

Leader's Guide

Heaven Can Wait (10–15 Minutes)

Obtain a copy of the movie *Heaven Can Wait*. (See the note on licensing on page 48.) Before showing the movie to your group, make sure each youth has permission from his or her parents. Show youth the scene where Warren Beatty rides his bike into a tunnel, is presumably hit and killed, and then appears in heaven. Ask:

- How does this movie portray heaven?
- What other movies have you seen that portray either heaven or hell? How do they compare to *Heaven Can Wait*?
- If you were making a movie about heaven, what would your heaven be like?
- Could heaven even be captured on film, or is it beyond human perception?

Say: "Christians have long believed not only in heaven, but also that God will somehow influence history or intervene in history to conquer all that is evil and bring about a perfect future. In this session, we will explore the idea of heaven and God's perfect future."

Make a Collage (14–18 minutes)

Divide the youth into groups of three or four. Give each group a poster board, newspapers, magazines, scissors, and glue. Ask the groups to create a collage with words and images related to heaven or God's future Kingdom. They may cut out full words and pictures, or they may use individual letters or words to build words or phrases.

Hand out student journals and ask youth to look at Visions of Heaven on pages 30–31. Also provide copies of the Afterlife in the Creeds handout from page 55. (You may also provide your denomination's statements of faith or words to "heavenly" hymns such as "When We All Get to Heaven" or "Swing Low, Sweet Chariot.") Ask the groups to look to these resources for ideas of images and words they could use in their collages. Also encourage them to use words and images from Scripture.

Do a Bible Survey (13–20 minutes)

Divide the class into six small groups, and assign each group one of the following Scriptures. (If you have a small number of youth, form two or three groups and assign each group two or three Scriptures.)

- **Matthew 19:16-30** (The rich young man)
- **Matthew 25:31-46** (The judgment of the nations)
- **Luke 16:19-31** (The rich man and Lazarus)
- **John 3:1-21** (Nicodemus visits Jesus)
- **1 Corinthians 13:8-13** (The gift of love)
- **Revelation 20:11—21:8** (The new heaven and the new earth)

Ask each group to look for words or phrases that describe the afterlife, tell what it takes to get to heaven, or say whether God will prevail in the end. Then have the groups look at the visions of heaven printed on pages 30–31 of the student journal. Ask them to find the description of heaven that best fits their assigned Scripture(s).

Ask one representative from each group to summarize their Scripture(s) and another to report on the group's findings. Record their findings on a board or large sheet of paper to keep track of which "vision of heaven" each group matched with its Scripture(s).

If youth have concerns regarding the doctrine of purgatory, explain that most Protestant denominations do not believe in purgatory because it is not mentioned or alluded to in Scripture.

Visions of Heaven (12–15 minutes)

i think i believe ...

Provide student journals and pens.

Ask each youth to read the various descriptions of heaven on pages 30–31 in the student journal. Have the youth underline the parts that make sense to them, and to cross out the parts they do not agree with. Then invite them to write their own brief descriptions of life after death.

Divide the youth into groups of two or three. Ask the groups to discuss their ideas and definitions of heaven and to talk about the "Questions to Ponder" on pages 28–29 of the student journal. Give each group a few minutes to present what they discussed and how they answered some of the questions. If time allows, ask individual youth to describe their versions of heaven.

Closing Worship (8–12 minutes)

lord, help me have faith

Provide Bibles and hymns or songbooks containing "Hymn of Promise." Other worship supplies and aids are optional.

Ask one or more of the youth to create an interpretive dance to accompany the hymn, "Hymn of Promise." Alternatively, a group of youth might physically interpret the words with hand motions or sign language. You may ask youth beforehand to prepare a dance or motions, or you may ask them to do an impromptu dance or improvise on the spot. Allow any youth who are interested to participate.

(If you cannot locate "Hymn of Promise," select another hymn that tells of God's promise of eternal life. If you select a different hymn, you will need to alter the questions below appropriately.)

Read aloud 1 Corinthians 13:8-13 and ask the youth to follow along in their Bibles. Then have them read or sing the verses of "Hymn of Promise" from a hymnal or songbook. Ask:

- What does it mean to say that what we see now is like a "dim image in a mirror"?
- What does "dim image in a mirror" suggest about doubts?
- Is it OK to be "fuzzy" about what happens to each person after death or how God will bring about God's kingdom?
- What do the images presented in "Hymn of Promise" say about death and life everlasting?

- What does the third verse of "Hymn of Promise" say about doubt?
- What do the hymn and the Scripture say about the relationship between doubt and faith?

Sing through "Hymn of Promise" while the volunteer performs his or her interpretive dance. If you have selected youth to interpret the lyrics with hand motions or sign language, run through the song once or twice, allowing these youth to teach the motions to the rest of the group.

Then, gather together in a circle and close with the following prayer or one of your own:

> Oh Lord, thank you for this life. We appreciate and thank you for the many gifts you've given us that we can experience here and now, such as friendship, faith, love, joy, and peace.
>
> Help us when we struggle with doubts and fears about what the future holds.
>
> Remind us that as long as you are with us—the same God who has given us so many good things in this life—that we can be sure that whatever you have in store for the future will be wonderful.
>
> Help us draw closer to you and your son, Jesus Christ, through the Holy Spirit, that we might experience on this earth a foretaste of our eternal lives in your presence. In Jesus' name we pray. Amen.

Notes on Video Viewing:

When you show home videocassettes or DVDs to a group of learners, you need to obtain a license. You can get a public performance license (sometimes called a site or umbrella license) from The Motion Picture Licensing Corporation's church desk at 800-515-8855.

The license is valid for twelve months and typically costs about $95. Check with your church to see if an umbrella license has already been obtained. Many denominations—through conferences, jurisdictions, dioceses, and other structures—secure licenses for their churches.

A Bad News/Good News Creed

Affirmation From Romans 8:35, 37-39

Leader:

Who shall separate us from the love of Christ?
Shall tribulation or distress,
or persecution or famine,
or nakedness or peril or sword?

People:

No!
In all things we are more than conquerors
through the one who loved us.
We are sure that neither
death nor life,
nor angels, nor principalities,
nor things present, nor things to come,
nor powers, nor height, nor depth,
nor anything else in all creation,
will be able to separate us from the love of God
in Christ Jesus our Lord.
Thanks be to God! Amen.

Write your own version of this creed, expressing in detail what you personally believe about the bad and good news. You can complete the responsive reading below, or rewrite the creed completely. Use the back side, if necessary.

Leader:

Who or what can separate us from the love of Christ?
Maybe …

People:

No!
Even though these things seem terrible
and can even make us doubt at times,
We believe …

Session 1 Reproducible Page

The Bible's Authority

Read and consider the following official church statements about the Bible. Then take a look at your church's official statement about the Bible.

- We believe in the Word of God contained in the Old and New Testaments as the sufficient rule both of faith and of practice. (*From "The Statement of Faith of the Korean Methodist Church"*)
- We believe the Holy Bible, Old and New Testaments, reveals the Word of God so far as it is necessary for our salvation. It is to be received through the Holy Spirit as the true rule and guide for faith and practice. Whatever is not revealed in or established by the Holy Scriptures is not to be made an article of faith nor is it to be taught as essential to salvation. (*Article IV from "The Confession of Faith of the Evangelical United Brethren Church"*)

Disagreement about the Bible

Read each pair of statements and circle the one you agree with more:

- Every word in the Bible should carry equal weight. If we ever say that one part of it is more important than another, then we are interpreting the Bible with our minds and are putting our brains above God's words.
- Since we know dinosaurs existed, and they are not recorded in the Bible, we can be sure that the Creation story is not complete from a scientific point of view. This omission means that the Bible was originally written as a book of faith so we shouldn't expect every chapter and every verse to be literally accurate.

- The Bible contains more than one point of view and not all of the biblical writers would have agreed with one another. This fact does not mean the Bible is contradictory; it just means that our faith is big enough to include different viewpoints.
- Every writer in the Bible would agree word-for-word with every other writer. Even the Old and New Testaments fit together like a hand and glove.

- The "Word of God" is Jesus. The ultimate authority in the Christian faith is Jesus Christ, who is revealed through the Bible, but who is above the Bible.
- The "Word of God" is the written Bible. The Bible itself is our real authority, like a book of laws God gave us to follow.

Match 'em up!

Read each Scripture listed below. The statements on the right are from various Christian creeds. After you read each Scripture, draw lines connecting it to any of the statements on the right that might have been inspired by that Scripture. It is OK for a Scripture or statement to have several lines going to it.

- **Matthew 28:19-20**
- **John 1:1-18**
- **John 14:8-20, 26**
- **Acts 2:1-33**
- **Galatians 5:16-25**
- **1 Peter 1:2**
- **2 Corinthians 13:13**
- **1 John 4:1-3**

- We believe in one God . . . maker of heaven and earth, of all that is, seen and unseen.
(*From "The Nicene Creed"*)
- I believe in God the Father Almighty, maker of heaven and earth.
(*From "The Apostles' Creed"*)
- We believe in God: who has created and is creating,
who has come in Jesus, the Word made flesh, to reconcile and make new, who works in us and others by the Spirit.
(*From "A Statement of Faith of the United Church of Canada"*)
- In life, in death, in life beyond death, God is with us. We are not alone.
(*From "A Statement of Faith of the United Church of Canada"*)
- We believe in Jesus Christ,
God manifest in the flesh, our teacher, example,
and Redeemer, the Savior of the world.
(*From "A Statement of Faith of the Korean Methodist Church"*)
- We believe in Jesus Christ, Son of God and Son of man,
the gift of the Father's unfailing grace, the ground of our hope,
and the promise of our deliverance from sin and death.
(*From "A Modern Affirmation"*)
- We believe in one Lord, Jesus Christ . . . of one Being with the Father . . .
for us and for our salvation he came down from heaven, was incarnate of the Holy Spirit and the Virgin Mary, and became truly human.
(*From "The Nicene Creed"*)
- We believe in the Holy Spirit, the Lord, the giver of life,
who proceeds from the Father and the Son . . .
(*From "The Nicene Creed"*)
- We believe in the Holy Spirit,
God present with us for guidance, for comfort, and for strength.
(*From "A Statement of Faith of the Korean Methodist Church"*)
- We believe in the Holy Spirit
as the divine presence in our lives,
whereby we are kept in perpetual remembrance of the truth of Christ,
and find strength and help in time of need.
(*From "A Modern Affirmation"*)

Metaphors for Jesus

John's Gospel uses several different metaphors that compare Jesus to something familiar to the people of his time and place. Look up the Scriptures below to see the many ways that Jesus is described in John's Gospel:

- **John 1:1-5** ______________________________
- **John 1:29** ______________________________
- **John 2:18-22** ______________________________
- **John 6:35** ______________________________
- **John 7:37-38** ______________________________
- **John 8:12, 9:5** ______________________________
- **John 9:35-37** ______________________________
- **John 10:7** ______________________________
- **John 10:11** ______________________________
- **John 11:25-26** ______________________________
- **John 14:6** ______________________________
- **John 15:1, 4-5** ______________________________
- **John 18:36-37, 19:18-22** ______________________________

Pretend Jesus came to your community today. Unless you have shepherds in your area, he would probably compare himself to something else in your area that would help people in your community understand him. Consider some of the possible metaphors listed below and answer the following questions:

- Which ones do you think Jesus might use? Which ones do you think make no sense?
- If Jesus used one of these metaphors, what do you think he would be saying about himself?
- What metaphor would you use to describe Jesus? Create your own.

A firefighter who runs into a burning building	A grocery store owner
A schoolteacher who cares for all of her or his students	A cellular phone
A lifeguard at a beach or a swimming pool	An emergency medical technician
A friend you talk to on instant messenger	A disk jockey at a dance
A writer of love songs	The Internet
The Library of Congress	A star in the sky
A seeing-eye dog	A cowboy riding a horse

Session 4 Reproducible Page

The Church in the Creeds

We believe in the one holy catholic* and apostolic church.
(*From "The Nicene Creed"*)

We are called to be the church:
to celebrate God's presence,
to love and serve others,
to seek justice and resist evil,
to proclaim Jesus, crucified and risen,
our judge and our hope.
(*From "A Statement of Faith of the United Church of Canada"*)

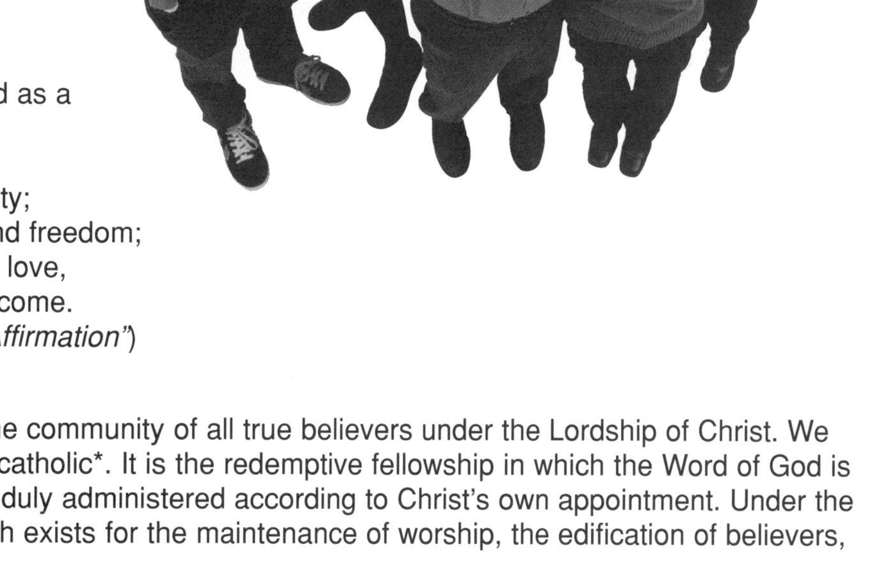

We believe in the church,
those who are united in the living Lord
for the purpose of worship and service.
We believe in the reign of God
as the divine will realized in human society,
and in the family of God,
where we are all brothers and sisters.
(*From "A Statement of Faith of the Korean Methodist Church"*)

Where the Spirit of the Lord is,
There is the one true church, apostolic and universal . . .
(*From "A Modern Affirmation"*)

We commit ourselves individually and as a community to the way of Christ:
to take up the cross;
to seek abundant life for all humanity;
to struggle for peace with justice and freedom;
to risk ourselves in faith, hope, and love,
praying that God's kingdom may come.
(*From "The World Methodist Social Affirmation"*)

We believe the Christian Church is the community of all true believers under the Lordship of Christ. We believe it is one, holy, apostolic, and catholic*. It is the redemptive fellowship in which the Word of God is preached . . . and the sacraments are duly administered according to Christ's own appointment. Under the discipline of the Holy Spirit the Church exists for the maintenance of worship, the edification of believers, and the redemption of the world.
(*From "The Confession of Faith of the Evangelical United Brethren Church"*)

* When "catholic church" is written with a lowercase *c*, it refers to the universal church of Christians everywhere and throughout time and not specifically the Roman Catholic Church.

Session 5 Reproducible Page

Life in the Creeds

The following statements come from various creeds, but they all have something to do with what Christians believe about life in this world. Circle those statements, or parts of statements, that you agree with. Cross out those statements, or parts of statements, that seem unrealistic to you. On the back, write anything that you would add to these statements.

In life, in death, in life beyond death,
God is with us.
We are not alone.
Thanks be to God. Amen.
(*From "A Statement of Faith of the United Church of Canada"*)

We believe in the forgiveness of sins,
in the life of love and prayer,
and in grace equal to every need.
(*From "A Statement of Faith of the Korean Methodist Church"*)

We believe in God . . .
whose mercy is over all his works,
and whose will is ever directed to his children's good.
We believe in Jesus Christ . . .
the ground of our hope,
and the promise of our deliverance from sin and death.
We believe in the Holy Spirit
as the divine presence in our lives,
whereby we are kept in perpetual remembrance of the truth of Christ,
and find strength and help in time of need.
We believe that this faith should manifest itself
in the service of love
as set forth in the example of our blessed Lord,
to the end
that the kingdom of God may come upon the earth. Amen.
(*From "A Modern Affirmation"*)

We rejoice in every sign of God's kingdom:
in the upholding of human dignity and community;
in every expression of love, justice, and reconciliation;
in each act of self-giving on behalf of others;
in the abundance of God's gifts entrusted to us that all may have enough;
in all responsible use of the earth's resources . . .
We commit ourselves individually and as a community to the way of Christ:
to take up the cross;
to seek abundant life for all humanity;
to struggle for peace with justice and freedom;
to risk ourselves in faith, hope, and love,
praying that God's kingdom may come.
(*From "The World Methodist Social Affirmation"*)

Session 6 Reproducible Page

Afterlife in the Creeds

The following statements come from various creeds, but they all have something to do with what Christians believe about life after death. Circle those statements, or parts of statements, that you agree with. Cross out those statements, or parts of statements, that seem unrealistic to you. On the back, write anything that you would add to these statements.

He will come again in glory to judge the living and the dead,
and his kingdom will have no end . . .
We look for the resurrection of the dead,
and the life of the world to come. Amen.
(From "The Nicene Creed")

In life, in death, in life beyond death, God is with us.
We are not alone.
Thanks be to God. Amen.
(From "A Statement of Faith of the United Church of Canada")

We believe in the final triumph of righteousness
and in the life everlasting.
(From "A Statement of Faith of the Korean Methodist Church")

We believe all men stand under the righteous judgment of Jesus Christ, both now and in the last day. We believe in the resurrection of the dead; the righteous to life eternal and the wicked to endless condemnation.
(From "The Confession of Faith of the Evangelical United Brethren Church")

Session 7 Reproducible Page

Appendix A

Read aloud the following statements based on well-known Bible narratives to the youth. Instruct each youth to hold up a number of fingers to indicate how strongly he or she believes each statement—a 1 represents sincere doubt, while a 10 represents total belief. (If some youth are uncomfortable holding up their fingers, allow them to put their hands under a table, behind their backs, or in their pockets.)

- **GOD CREATED THE HEAVENS AND THE EARTH.**
- **ADAM AND EVE SINNED, DISRUPTING GOD'S PERFECT CREATION.**
- **GOD DESTROYED THE WORLD WITH A GREAT FLOOD, SAVING ONLY NOAH'S FAMILY AND SELECT ANIMALS.**
- **GOD APPEARED TO MOSES IN A BURNING BUSH.**
- **MOSES PARTED THE RED SEA AND PEOPLE WALKED THROUGH ON DRY LAND.**
- **GOD SPOKE DIRECTLY TO THE PROPHETS, SO THEY WOULD KNOW EXACTLY WHAT TO SAY TO THE PEOPLE.**
- **JESUS WAS BORN.**
- **VISITORS FROM THE EAST FOLLOWED A STAR TO FIND OUT WHERE JESUS WAS BORN.**
- **JESUS HEALED MANY PEOPLE, INCLUDING A MAN WHO WAS BORN BLIND.**
- **JESUS WALKED ON WATER.**
- **JESUS ROSE FROM THE DEAD.**
- **JESUS IS THE MESSIAH, THE SON OF GOD.**
- **JESUS CAME INTO THE WORLD, NOT TO JUDGE AND SCOLD PEOPLE, BUT TO SAVE PEOPLE FROM THEIR SINS AND GIVE THEM ETERNAL LIFE.**
- **ALL PEOPLE ARE SINNERS, AND HAVE DONE THINGS THAT DISAPPOINT GOD.**
- **IF WE SIN, NO MATTER HOW TERRIBLE IT MAY SEEM TO BE, GOD IS ABLE AND WILLING TO FORGIVE IT COMPLETELY, ONCE AND FOR ALL, WHEN WE ASK GOD TO FORGIVE US.**
- **JESUS LOVES EACH ONE OF YOU, AND IS STILL YOUR FRIEND TODAY.**

Appendix B: Jesus' Life Timeline

The following statements about Jesus' life story are listed in the proper order. Write each on a separate index card. (Key events are in boldface.)

- John the Baptist was born.
- **Jesus was born.**
- Angels appeared to the shepherds to announce Jesus' birth.
- Jesus worked as a carpenter.
- John the Baptist began preaching in the wilderness and baptizing people.
- **Jesus was baptized by John the Baptist.**
- Jesus was tempted in the wilderness by Satan but resisted temptation.
- **Jesus asked some fishermen and others to become his disciples.**
- Jesus preached the famous "Sermon on the Mount."
- Jesus miraculously fed a crowd of 5000 even though there was not enough food.
- Jesus walked on water.
- Jesus told the parables of the sower, the mustard seed, and the hidden treasure.
- Jesus healed a man born blind.
- Jesus raised Lazarus from the dead.
- Judas Iscariot betrayed Jesus.
- **Jesus had the last supper with his disciples.**
- Jesus was put on trial, mocked, and flogged.
- Peter denied ever knowing Jesus.
- **Jesus was crucified, giving his life for the forgiveness of our sins.**
- **Jesus was raised from the dead, and appeared to his female disciples and then to the Eleven.**
- Thomas, a disciple, refused to believe Jesus' resurrection until he saw and touched Jesus himself.
- **Jesus was taken up into heaven.**
- Jesus spoke to Saul, a persecutor of Christians, converting him to Paul, a great Christian leader.
- The books of Matthew, Mark, Luke, and John were written about Jesus.

Write each of the following false statements on a separate index card and mix them with the true statements above. Some are funny, while others are a little tricky. Add your own if you wish.

- Before becoming a preacher, Jesus was very successful working with his dad as a used car salesman.
- Jesus overruled a referee's bad call in a key play in the first World Series, giving the "Angels" the win.
- Jesus invented chocolate, bringing joy to people everywhere.
- Jesus' disciple, Santa, was the first ever to safely go down a chimney in Jerusalem.
- The wise men followed a star, probably Tom Cruise or some other star, down a yellow brick road to find his way to the Wizard of Oz.
- Jesus was found floating in a basket in a river by a Princess, and later parted the Red Sea with a loud command and series of hand claps.
- Jesus wrote the book of Romans warning the Romans not to attack the Jewish people.
- Jesus began keeping a list of children everywhere to keep track of who is naughty and who is nice.
- Jesus was swallowed by a whale, but was later safely spit out on land.
- Jesus found the Ten Commandments written on stone tablets on top of a mountain.
- Jesus gathered up all the animals of the world, two by two, and put them on the ark.

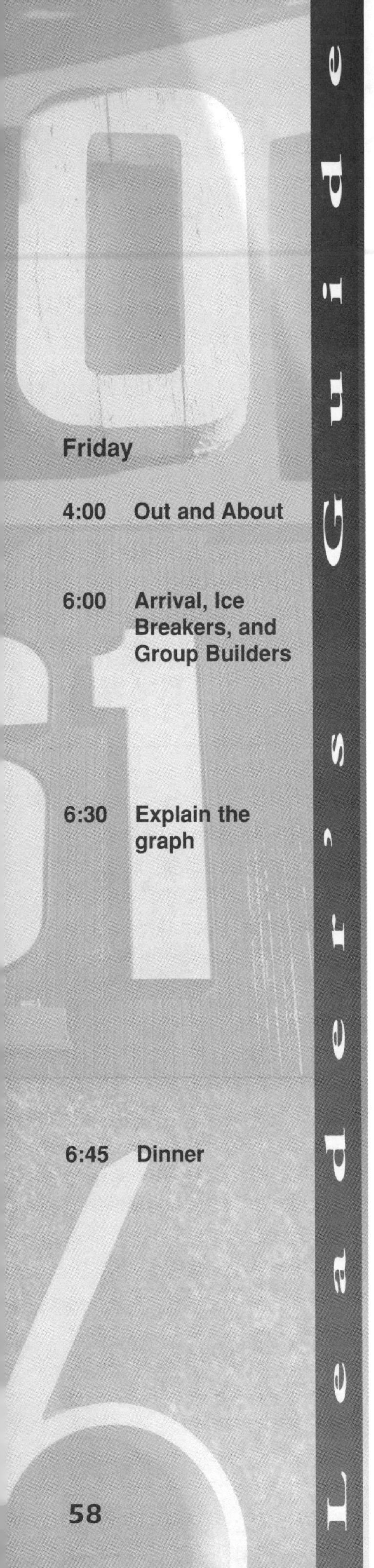

Friday

4:00 Out and About

6:00 Arrival, Ice Breakers, and Group Builders

6:30 Explain the graph

6:45 Dinner

I Think, I Wonder, I Believe Retreat

Purpose: To help youth examine and affirm their basic Christian beliefs

Preparation: Provide plenty of paper and writing utensils. Obtain the necessary supplies for the craft project and the movie (both on page 60). Review the worship service on pages 61–62, the out and about on pages 63–64, and the appropriate activities from Sessions Two through Seven.

Friday

If time allows, do Out and About: Visit a Christian Bookstore from pages 61–62 on your way to your retreat destination Friday afternoon.

Arrival, Ice Breakers, and Group Builders

Once you arrive at your destination, give youth time to unpack and settle in. If needed, spend play some ice breaking and group building games—such as Play Bible Games from page 16—to help everyone feel comfortable and begin to form new relationships with one another.

The "Beliefs—Sort 'em Out!" Graph

Enlist volunteers to help you cover a wall or table top with large sheets of paper to make a giant version of the graph printed below. (Be sure the paper is thick enough that markers won't bleed through it onto the wall or table.)

	God	Jesus, Holy Spirit	Sin, Salva–tion	The Church	Life on Earth	Life After Death
The Bible Says . . .						
The Creeds Say . . .						
I Believe . . .						

After each short lesson (such as We Believe the Bible or We Believe in God), encourage individuals or small groups to fill in the corresponding squares on the graph. Make the task of completing the graph a focal point of the retreat.

When you introduce and explain the graph, give each youth a unique color of highlighter, marker, colored pencil, crayon, or pen that will be his or her color for the duration of the retreat. Whenever there is spare time, encourage youth to add comments and underline or highlight meaningful phrases in their own unique color. Allow youth to post questions for discussion—and to respond to questions that have been posted—beside the graph at any point during the retreat.

We Believe the Bible

Do the following activities from Session Two (We Believe the Bible):

- Should You Throw Away an Old Bible? (page 16)
- Here I Stand (page 18)
- I Believe; Help My Unbelief! (page 18)

Add Posters to the Room

Distribute copies of pages 51, 53, 54, and 55 or provide creeds or statements of faith commonly used by your denomination or congregation. Instruct youth to make posters illustrating key Christian beliefs, using the creeds and statements of faith as a guide.

Optional Late Evening Activity: Listen to contemporary Christian music. Ask youth to select a song that they think conveys a meaningful Christian message. Invite individuals or small groups to create an interpretive dance or piece of art based on the song and encourage them to present it to the rest of the group.

Saturday

We Believe in God

Do the following activities from Session Three (We Believe in God):

- Match Scriptures with the Creeds (page 23)
- Make a Poster Series (page 23)
- Lord, Is It a Sin to Doubt You? (page 24)

We Believe in Jesus Christ

Do the following activities from Session Four (We Believe in Jesus Christ):

- Jesus' Life Timeline (page 28)
- Consult the Creeds (page 28)
- Continue Consult the Creeds (page 28)
- Who is Jesus to You? (page 29)

We Believe in Living This Life

Do the following activities from Session Six (We Believe in Living This Life):

- Rank the World's Problems (page 34)
- Color-Code the Creeds (page 35)
- Create Your Own Creed (page 36)

7:30 Activities from Session Two

8:30 Add Posters to the Room

9:00 Break and/or optional activities

10:00 Snack

10:15 Evening devotion

11:00 Lights Out

Saturday

7:30 Breakfast

9:00 Activities from Session Three

10:15 Break

10:30 Activities from Session Four

11:45 Break

12:00 Lunch

12:45 Your choice of games, activities, or free time

2:00 Activities from Session Six

3:15 Craft Project

5:00 Dinner

6:00 Activities from Session Seven

7:30 Watch and Discuss the Movie

Consider serving refreshments such as soft drinks and popcorn during the movie and discussion.

10:00 Devotion and group singing

12:00 Lights out

Sunday

8:00 Breakfast

9:00 Activities from Session Five

Leader's Guide

Craft project

Using felt (or other cloth suitable for a large banner), make an "I Believe" banner or banner series expressing the main themes (Scripture, God, Christ, and so on) of the Christian faith. The entire group could create one large banner, or several small groups could each create a banner representing a different theme. The banners might include phrases from creeds, Bible verses, or Christian symbols. Encourage them to be creative and to feature plenty of color. If all goes well, the finished project could be taken home and displayed in your church.

We Believe in Eternal Life

Do the following activities from Session Seven (We Believe in Eternal Life):

- Make a Collage (page 46)
- Do a Bible Survey (pages 46–47)
- Visions of Heaven (page 47)

Watch and Discuss *Places in the Heart.*

Be sure to collect permission forms from each youth, signed by his or her parent or guardian. Also, see the note on permissions on page 62.

Show the movie *Places in the Heart*, and ask youth to pay attention to what causes relationships between the characters to draw closer or drift apart. Following the movie ask:

- In the movie, which relationships were damaged by sin? How did sin affect these relationships?
- Were any of these damaged relationships healed? If so, how?
- How does the final scene in this movie relate both to living this life and to God's final victory? What signs or changes occur in the final scene to indicate that it is meant to portray God's final victory? What are your feelings about this portrayal?
- Compare the final scene of this movie to Revelation 21:1-6. In the movie what has been "made new"?

Following the discussion, lead a group devotion on Revelation 21:1-6.

Sunday

We Believe in the Church

Do the following activities from Session Five (We Believe in the Church):

- Balloon Creeds (pages 34–35)
- Top Ten Purposes of the Church (pages 35–36)
- Make a Paper Chain (page 36)
- Explore "We Are the Church" (page 36)

Sunday Morning Worship

Do the Worship in an Eggshell service from pages 61–62. Modify the songs and prayers as appropriate for your group and setting.

Select or create a special setting for worship. If possible, have it prepared where the youth cannot see it, and then lead them all to it. It may be an outdoor pavilion, an indoor chapel, or a section of the room that you have set aside as worship space.

Use any of the banners or posters the youth have created as your backdrop. You may wish to include a cross and candles.

10:00	**Break or group singing**
10:30	**Sunday morning worship**
11:30	**Lunch**
12:00	**Pack and load vehicles**
1:00	**Depart**

Worship in an Eggshell

- **The Breaking of the Eggs:** Obtain numerous multicolored plastic eggs. Label each egg with a permanent marker, so you can refer to the eggs as "red egg #1," "blue egg #2," and so on.

  Place an instruction for the worship service inside each egg. Most of the instructions should be serious, but include some fun surprises.You may open the eggs in a particular order or a random order. (If you open the eggs in a random order, keep the instructions for the opening and closing of the service separate). Here are some sample instructions you might write out and place inside the eggs:

Stand up, stretch your arms up high, and say, "Good morning, God! Thank you for this day."	Sing a song of praise to God—choose your favorite!
Read Psalm 103:1-13.	Sing any hymn or Christian song you choose.
If your birthday is in the spring, stand, switch places with someone, and greet your new neighbors.	Invite the group to join hands and recite together the Lord's Prayer.
Complete the sentence: "In this life, Christians should _____." Invite others to complete the sentence.	Invite everyone to complete the sentence: "God, remember _____. It is a big problem right now."

Include several instructions that give youth an opportunity to reflect on what they believe about God, Jesus, the Holy Spirit, the Bible, the church, this life, and life eternal.

Gather everyone in a circle, and scatter the eggs among the group. Have the youth pass and roll the eggs around the circle for a few seconds. Then call out an egg color and number. The person with that egg should open it and announce what the next part of worship will be. In many cases the person opening the egg will be asked to lead that portion of worship in some way. After that part of the service has been

If certain youth are uncomfortable with this activity, allow them to pass their eggs to someone else or to you.

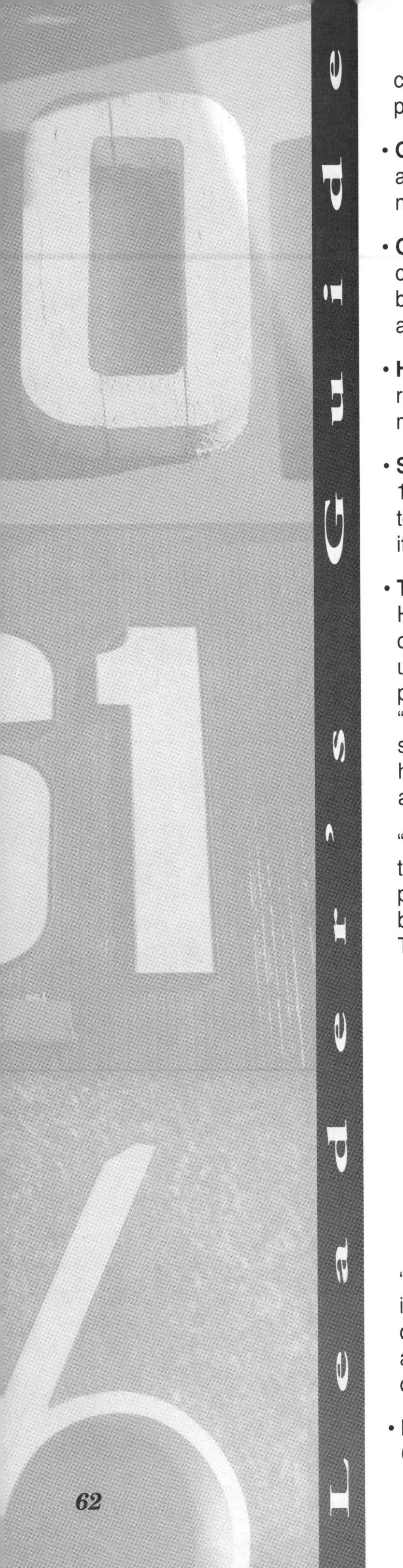

completed, that egg should be removed from the circle. Repeat this process until all the eggs have been opened.

- **Group Hug:** Have everyone stand, move in close for a "group hug," and then say together, "We believe in the church. We believe people need God, and one another."

- **Giving Thanks for One Another:** Join hands, then go around the circle, inviting each participant offer a one-sentence prayer of thanks or blessing for the person to his or her right. Continue praying by letting anyone offer a prayer of concern or thanksgiving.

- **Hymn of Community:** Sing "We are the Church" or another hymn that refers to the community of believers. Invite youth to create hand motions or an interpretive dance. (You should arrange this beforehand.)

- **Scripture:** Gather youth in a circle and select one youth to read aloud 1 Corinthians 12:12-19, 27. Go around the circle, allowing each person to say something about what these verses mean to him or her, or what it means for him or her to be part of the church through this group.

- **The Ceremony of the Yarn:** Give a large ball of yarn to one youth. Have that youth hold the end of the yarn, and roll the ball across the circle to another youth. This person will hold onto the yarn that has unraveled and roll the ball of yarn to another youth. Each time, the person who rolls the yarn should say to the person receiving the yarn, "You are part of Christ's body." The person receiving the yarn should say, "You are part of Christ's body too." Continue until everyone is holding onto the yarn. Sing, "We are one in the Spirit" or another song about oneness in Christ. While youth are connected by the yarn, say:

  "Even though we are many different individuals, the church ties us together in one community. Just as we passed the yarn from one person to another, we become a part of the church when we are invited by someone else. In turn, we invite others to be part of the community. The yarn symbolizes that which binds us together, such as:

  1) Faith: By worshiping together in the church and sharing our faith in Jesus Christ, we are tied together in one community.

  2) Hope: This yarn that everyone can hold and extend to anyone else symbolizes the church's goal to look beyond external differences such as age, race, nationality, handicapping conditions, and economic status. This gives us hope.

  3) Love: This yarn symbolizes the love that Christians have receive from God through Jesus Christ, the love Christians have for one another, and the love that Christians can share with the world.

  "This yarn is just a ball of yarn, but it symbolizes something much more important. I will cut the yarn so that you can keep a piece in your Bible, or somewhere else where you will see it. It will remind you that you are a part of the church and are therefore a part of the faith, hope, and love of Jesus Christ." Cut the yarn so that each of you can take a piece.

- **Holy Communion:** If it is possible and desirable, conclude with Holy Communion.

Out and About: Visit a Christian Bookstore

Copy the Shopping List handout from page 64. Contact a local Christian bookstore and ask the manager if he or she would have any problems with your group visiting the store and doing this activity. Offer to come at a time when the store is not usually very busy. Before taking your group to the store, visit the store yourself to get an idea of the layout and the types of products for sale.

Select a time to take your youth to this store. Distribute copies of the Shopping List handout from page 64 and pens or pencils. Ask the youth to complete the activity individually. Instruct them to record on the handout the items they selected from the store and their answers to the questions. Set a time to meet at the front of the store before you leave. Gather afterward at another store for a ceremonial ice cream cone! Allow youth to report and discuss their answers.

Then ask the following questions:

- Did the store we visited emphasize the Christian beliefs YOU think are important? Why or why not?
- What would you add more of if you were in charge of this store? Do you think the products you would add would sell as well as the others? Why or why not?
- Why do you think some beliefs are more popular, or marketable, than others?
- What Scriptures posted in the store did you find most meaningful? (See the bottom of the Shopping List handout.) Why?
- Which pictures of Jesus best matched what you think Jesus looked like? (See the bottom of the Shopping List handout.) Why?

One item on the handout instructs the youth to select a CD featuring Christian songs that tell stories and that lend themselves to motions and interpretive dance. Before leaving the store consider purchasing one of the CDs recommended by the youth. This could come in handy for worship services or for the Optional Late Night Activity on page 59.

Notes on Video Viewing:

When you show home videocassettes or DVDs to a group of learners, you need to obtain a license. You can get a public performance license (sometimes called a site or umbrella license) from The Motion Picture Licensing Corporation's church desk at 800-515-8855. The license is valid for twelve months and typically costs about $95. Check with your church to see if an umbrella license has already been obtained. Many denominations—through conferences, jurisdictions, dioceses, and other structures—secure licenses for their churches.

Shopping List

Find the one book, besides the Bible, that you think would best explain the Christian faith to a teenager.

Find one item you would give to a five year-old child who did not go to church to show that child that Jesus loves him or her.

Pick a place in the store to stand. Listen and look around. What can you see or hear that indicates to you that this is a Christian store?

Look at the collection of music. Find one CD that might have story-type songs that your group could use to create dramatic interpretations for worship or for use in Sunday school or youth fellowship. (You might ask a salesperson for a recommendation.)

Find one item that would offer a message of encouragement and faith to someone who is going through a rough time. What message would this item send, and how might it help?

Look at the gift items (such as figurines, metal crosses, and so on). Find two or three items that express some of the main beliefs of the Christian faith. Why did you choose these items?

Next to each item below write "a lot," "quite a few," "just a few," or "none," to indicate how many gifts, books, or items in the store express each Christian belief:

- Christians should praise and worship God. ________
- Christians should share their faith with others. ________
- Christians should be concerned with protecting the environment (God's creation). ________
- Christians should accept Jesus Christ as their Lord an Savior and put him first in their lives. ________
- Christians should feed the hungry, shelter the homeless, and help the poor. ________
- Christians should love one another, regardless of differences such as physical conditions, race, age, or wealth. ________
- Christians should love even their enemies. ________
- Christians should care for the sick and visit those who are in prison. ________
- Christians should take Communion and be baptized. ________
- Christians should read and learn about the Bible. ________

Of all the sayings and Scriptures posted in the store, which is most meaningful to you?

Of all the pictures of Jesus you see in the store, which best matches what you think Jesus looked like?

On a scale from *1* (poor) to *10* (excellent), how well does the store give the impression that Christianity is a faith for people of all ages, nations, races, and abilities?

Out and About Reproducible Page